WOMEN WHO WOULD BE KINGS

Female Rulers of the Sixteenth Century

WOMEN WHO WOULD BE KINGS
Female Rulers of the Sixteenth Century

by

Lisa Hopkins

VISION PRESS · LONDON
ST. MARTIN'S PRESS · NEW YORK

Vision Press Ltd.
c/o Vine House Distribution
Waldenbury, North Common
Chailey, E. Sussex BN8 4DR

and

St. Martin's Press, Inc.
175 Fifth Avenue
New York
N.Y. 10010

ISBN (UK) 0 85478 307 5
ISBN (US) 0 312 06595 7

Library of Congress Cataloging-in-Publication Data
Hopkins, Lisa, 1962–
  Women who would be kings: female rulers of the sixteenth
century/ by Lisa Hopkins.
  ISBN 0-312-06595-7
  1. Europe—Kings and rulers—Biography. 2. Europe—Queens—
Biography. 3. Europe—History—1494–1648. I. Title.
D226.7.H67   1991
940.2'2'092—dc20
[B]   91-13696
                                                  CIP

**For my aunt and uncle
and my grandmother**

Printed and bound in Great Britain by
Billing & Sons, Worcester.
Typeset by Galleon Photosetting,
Ipswich, Suffolk.
MCMXCI

Contents

INTRODUCTION:

Women Rulers Before the Sixteenth Century

IN sixteenth-century Europe a woman was regarded as naturally, inherently and unalterably inferior to a man. This view was a very old one, and as a result the societies of Europe had evolved a whole host of legal, cultural, social and political practices which were specifically designed to ensure that that unstable, disorderly, untrustworthy creature, woman, was firmly subordinated to the guidance and guardianship of a man. The law accorded women no status in their own right, categorizing them all as either married or about to be married, and giving their husbands full control over all their property unless such control had already been assigned by their fathers to other male trustees. Medicine stressed that women's bodies made them subject to extremes of emotion; theology and, frequently, literature pointed out that it had been Eve, the first woman, who had been the primary cause of Adam's sin and thus of the Fall of Man; and society reprimanded women who strayed outside their traditional rôles by burning them as witches or subjecting them to the humiliation of a *charivari*. This was a ceremony enacted in small communities which could take different forms in different countries and at different times, but which always hinged on the holding up to public ridicule of those members of the community who were held to have deviated from the norm in sexual matters, whether by contracting an unsuitable marriage, straying from the marriage bed, or not adhering to the rôles traditionally allotted to the sexes. Thus, where a husband was considered not to be doing his proper job of keeping his wife in order, the local community might well step in to do it for him.

Such intervention to curb deviation could be easily justified to the sixteenth-century mind. It would not appear as an infringement of individual rights, for in sixteenth-century Europe people were seen less as individuals than as parts of a complex network of hierarchical relationships which governed and determined the whole fabric of society. The structure of society could be thought of as a pyramid: at the bottom, the masses; above them, where the triangle began to thin out, the less numerous gentry and nobility; and at the very apex of the triangle, the culminating figure of all, the King himself. Such an idea both described social realities during the period—there were indeed far more people at the bottom of the pile than at the top, and the power of the King, in some countries, could be very great indeed—and also offered a palliation of them, since it implied that everyone, no matter how apparently insignificant, had a proper place within the pyramid and, by their very existence, helped to confirm its shape and to keep it in being. Further comfort was offered to those in the lower echelons of the social order by the idea prevalent during the period that the King was not only the anointed deputy of God but was also, like God, a father-figure, who exercised over his subjects not an arbitrary and tyrannical power but a benevolent, paternal relationship directed towards their own best interests. The relationship between the King and his subjects was, indeed, a close parallel to that between a husband and his wife: each had been appointed by God to be in a position of authority over the other by virtue of superior strength, virtue and wisdom.

As the sixteenth century wore on, however, this patriarchal structure began to be increasingly challenged by a sudden and serious shortage of Kings. Henry VIII in England, James V in Scotland, Ferdinand and Isabella in Spain and Henry d'Albret in Navarre all failed to produce sons who lived to maturity, and so for a long time did Philip II of Spain. Dynastic continuity was vital for stability; without it there would almost certainly be civil war, so where there were no sons, there was no alternative but for a daughter to succeed. And so the chances of birth, marriage and death amongst its royal families brought to sixteenth-century Europe a rash of countries ruled not by Kings but by Queens.

There was already one woman ruler—Isabella of Castile, who by 1500 had been Queen of Castile in her own right for

8

twenty-six years and Queen consort of her husband's kingdom of Aragon for twenty-one. When she died in 1504, she was succeeded as Queen of Castile by her daughter, Juana; and though Juana herself never really exercised power, she was soon to be followed by other Queens who did: in Scotland by Mary, Queen of Scots; in England briefly and ill-fatedly by Lady Jane Grey and, much more permanently, by Mary of England and her sister Elizabeth; and in the tiny Pyreneean country of Navarre by Jeanne d'Albret. Nor were these Queens regnant the only women to exercise gubernatorial power: in Scotland, Mary of Guise ruled as Regent for her daughter Mary, Queen of Scots, while in Spain and the Netherlands the accumulation of territories far removed from each other, both by geography and custom, was to leave both the Habsburg King-Emperor Charles V and his son and successor Philip with a pressing need for deputies to govern for them those parts of their vast possessions which they could not personally superintend, and with a simultaneous shortage of reliable male relations who could be used in this demanding and difficult task. Their solution was to turn to the female members of their families, a policy which made Isabella of Portugal Regent of Spain during periods when her husband was absent and which also produced four female Governors of the Netherlands: Margaret of Austria, Mary of Hungary, Margaret of Parma and the Infanta Isabella Clara Eugenia. Finally, even the arch-bastion of male rule, France—where the Salic law meant that no woman could ever succeed—knew periods of female government: Louise of Savoy acted as Regent during the imprisonment of her son Francis I, in the earlier part of the century, and in the later half, the Queen Mother Catherine de' Medici superintended the minority of her son King Charles IX.

The fact that so many women were able to exercise such authority during the sixteenth century may be taken to suggest that there were in fact very few obstacles lying in the way of women rulers. But those who succeeded in wielding power need to be seen against a backdrop of those who failed to do so and who often paid a terrible price for such failure; and even amongst those who actually reached the pinnacles of power there was a high rate of unhappiness and failure. Mary of Guise and Mary of England both died in the knowledge that the religion to which they personally were committed was a lost cause in the country which they ruled, and Mary of England had to suffer the additional burden of knowing that this was directly due to her own inability to produce a child. Her sister Elizabeth had also to contend with childlessness, and indeed did not feel able even to take a husband, while other royal women like Lady Margaret Douglas, Lady Arabella Stuart, and Lady Mary and Lady Catherine Grey were all unable to gain approval for marriages with the men of their choice. Lady Jane Grey, the sister of Lady Catherine and Lady Mary, had a husband she did not want foisted upon her and was then forced to become an unwilling pawn in the political machinations of his family, for which she had to pay with her head at the age of 16. Lady Jane was only one of several royal women to die on the block in the sixteenth century: Henry VIII's second and fifth wives, Anne Boleyn and Catherine Howard, both lost their heads, and so did Margaret, Countess of Salisbury, niece of a King, and Mary, Queen of Scots, a Queen in her own right, while Juana of Castile spent almost the whole of her reign confined for insanity. The price of both failure and success could, for powerful women, be very high indeed.

Small wonder that some women of the period actually turned down the position of Queen: Margaret of Austria said she would rather remain a widow than marry Henry VII of England, and her niece Christina of Denmark similarly refused to marry Henry VII's son, Henry VIII, on the grounds that she wanted to keep her head safe on her shoulders. When Henry VIII did eventually find a fourth wife in Anne of Cleves, she was only too pleased to be divorced after six months of matrimony, and firmly resisted all attempts by her brother to persuade her to return to Cleves and to the possibility of a second marriage. Lady Frances Brandon renounced her own rights to the throne in favour of her daughter Jane, as a result of which she herself survived the rebellion which cost her daughter and husband their heads, and Elizabeth of York proved happy to renounce her own possible claim to the throne and to take her place instead as Queen consort of her husband, Henry VII.

This passivity on the part of Elizabeth of York made her a member of the most numerous group of women whose stories will be considered here: Queens consort, women who exercised little or no political power and whose primary functions were to bring their husbands dowries or to transmit land, to act as seals of alliances and to bear children. This was the normal, the traditional rôle of the Queen, and throughout the sixteenth century there were, as there had been for hundreds of years past, many women who still fulfilled it. They and their histories will play a considerable part when taking into account the rôle of queenship in the sixteenth century. But before any assessment can be made of that rôle and of how it did or did not alter during the course of the century, it is first of all necessary to attempt a brief survey of the sort of precedents of queenship which already existed at the outset of the century.

Educated men and women of the period would be well aware that the rule of women was by no means a new thing. The humanism which was spreading from Italy and gradually reaching the rest of Europe had encouraged a greater familiarity with classical writers, and even the most cursory acquaintance with such authors as Tacitus or Plutarch would introduce the reader to the stories of powerful women like Cleopatra in Egypt and Boadicea in Britain. The histories of these two women as told by classical authors, however, would not only introduce the reader to the idea of women ruling; they would also impress on his or her mind the fact that the careers both of Cleopatra and of Boadicea had ended in spectacular failure for themselves and for their kingdoms, and that in each case it was their femininity which had made them specially vulnerable. The cowardice supposedly innate in women had caused Cleopatra to flee from the battle of Actium, and Antony, her lover, had been foolish enough to turn and follow her, leading to the loss of the battle and their suicides—a story from which it was very easy to draw the moral that a noble man had been ruined by a passion for an over-emotional, weak woman.

The story of Boadicea could yield similar evidence for the unsuitability of women to rule. Boadicea's husband, the King of the Iceni, had had no son, and so had wished to transmit his kingdom to his daughters rather than have it absorbed by Rome. When the Roman governor of Britain attempted to disregard his wish, Boadicea led the Iceni in a rebellion against the Romans, but was defeated and died, probably at her own hand, soon after. Even before the rebellion, she herself had been flogged in punishment for attempting to assert what she saw as her rights—and her daughters, at some stage either before, during or after the rebellion, were raped. This meant that their honour had been lost and, since there would be uncertainty about the paternity of any children they might bear, their status as transmitters of an inheritance was seriously compromised. This attempt forcibly to sully the Icenian blood-line could be taken as underlining the vulnerability of female rulers—a vulnerability which seems to have been savagely confirmed in the fifteenth century, when Caterina Sforza was raped by her captor Cesare Borgia, and again in the sixteenth century if, as seems probable, Mary, Queen of Scots was indeed raped by the Earl of Bothwell as a means of forcing her into marriage with him.

Indeed, it was the question of female chastity—or, as it often seemed to the mediaeval and Renaissance mind, the innate absence of any such quality in the female make-up—which lay at the heart of the question of women rulers. Juana II of Naples, who had succeeded her brother Ladislas in 1414, had been notorious for her lovers, and was taken as an example of what women in power were only too likely to do; and it was also the issue of female fidelity which was the root of the most famous of all debates about the status of women rulers, the question of the Salic Law. This law, invoked in France after the death in 1316 of both Louis X and his son John I, was to be a bone of contention for years and was the direct cause of the Hundred Years' War between England and France; and yet in fact it arose not from any fixed considerations of principle, but as an urgent response to a pressing practical situation.

King Louis had, unfortunately for both himself and France, been plagued with marital difficulties. To contemporaries, this did not seem surprising: for Louis and both of his brothers were, after all, cursed. Their father, King Philip the Fair, had burned alive the Grandmaster of the Knights

Templar, Jacques de Molay, and when tied to the stake de Molay had pronounced a curse on Philip the Fair and on all his heirs to the thirteenth generation. That curse certainly seemed to be fulfilled in King Louis. He had been married to Marguerite of Burgundy, and since Burgundy was both a near neighbour of France and a potential thorn in her side, both of his two brothers, Philip and Charles, had also been married to daughters of Burgundy, cousins of Marguerite: Jeanne, who married the elder brother Philip, and Blanche, who married the younger one, Charles. Thus Philip the Fair had succeeded in finding brides for all three of his sons. He had also, however, a daughter, Isabella. She was married not into the ducal family of Burgundy but to a King of England, Edward II; and it is said to have been she who first spotted that all was not well with her brothers' marriages, and alerted her father to the fact. A watch was set on the three princesses and it was soon established that the unthinkable had taken place. Both Marguerite and Blanche were having affairs, and Jeanne was helping them.

The repercussions of this were tremendous. The lovers of Marguerite and Blanche were tried and hideously executed, and the adulterous princesses themselves were imprisoned in the old and uncomfortable fortress of Château-Gaillard, while Jeanne, since she had not actually been guilty of adultery herself, was confined in slightly less uncomfortable circumstances at Dourdan. Punishing the offenders, however, did nothing to solve the terrible problem that their offence had created: not one of the three women had presented their husbands with a son. Therefore none of the three brothers had a male heir, and, worse still, while they were married to women who were imprisoned they had no chance of fathering legitimate offspring. The eldest brother, Louis, had indeed had a daughter, Jeanne, by his wife Marguerite of Burgundy, but that if anything made the situation worse rather than better, for the revelation that the child's mother had had an affair had of course laid her paternity open to question, and the crown of France could not possibly be allowed to pass to someone who might not be the legitimate heir.

There remained two possible options open to the three

princes: they could hope that their wives would die, or they could attempt to obtain divorces from them. However, neither of these options could be easily realized. Imprisonment in the old fortress of Château-Gaillard might well have been expected to produce a deterioration in the princesses' health, but unfortunately for their husbands both of them held up well under the harsh conditions of their confinement and obstinately refused to sicken and die. Divorce proved equally problematic. Divorces could be granted only by the Pope, and the papacy was at the time in a state of considerable disarray: arguments within the church and interference by secular rulers had led to the removal of the popes from Rome, and they were currently established in Avignon, in southern France. The new location was by no means universally approved of, and the papacy was at a low ebb in terms of authority, vigour and power. Even worse, at the time when Louis, the eldest of the three French princes, was manoeuvring for a divorce, the most recent Pope had just died and the conclave of cardinals was having difficulty electing a successor—and until a new pope was elected there could be no possibility of a divorce, for there was no one in existence who could grant one.

Small wonder that when Marguerite of Burgundy did in fact die at Château-Gaillard, shortly after King Philip the Fair had died and her husband had succeeded him as King Louis X, rumours were rife that her death was not due to natural causes and that she had in fact been strangled. Whatever the truth of that, Louis was certainly quick enough to marry again, choosing as his second wife Clemency of Hungary. Clemency was the daughter of a poor and exiled family, and perhaps Louis thought she would be sufficiently grateful for her sudden elevation to refrain from the kind of antics her predecessor had indulged in, and would manage to provide him with a legitimate male heir of unquestionable parentage.

King Louis' hopes were to be fulfilled; but he himself did not live to see it. In 1316, only two years after coming to the throne, he died, his death being attributed by many contemporaries to the curse of the dead Grandmaster de Molay. At the time of his death the Queen was pregnant; and

France held its breath, for if she produced a son, then there need be no problem about the succession, whereas if Queen Clemency's child was a daughter, then it would be necessary to decide whether the throne should pass to the new baby, to Marguerite of Burgundy's daughter Jeanne, or, on some pretext, to neither.

To everyone's relief, the baby was indeed a boy, and was duly pronounced King John I of France. But almost immediately the baby followed its father to the grave—a victim of the Templar curse, said some; poisoned, said others, by its godmother Mahaut of Artois, whose son-in-law might well become the next King after his baby nephew's death; not dead at all, said a third group, but swapped in his cradle with an Italian banker's son, who maintained until his dying day that he was in fact the rightful King of France. But to the nobles of France the cause of the baby's death was much less important than its effects, for they now found themselves faced with a terrible dilemma. Should they accept as their Queen the little Jeanne, the daughter that Marguerite of Burgundy had borne while she was still the wife of King Louis X, and simply overlook the doubts about her parentage; or should they opt for the late King's eldest brother Philip, a mature man of unquestioned descent, and decide to risk whatever manifestations of displeasure might come from the Duke of Burgundy, the uncle of the small Jeanne?

In the event, they chose the latter course; a grown-up son of Philip the Fair seemed a more attractive choice than a girl-child who might or might not be the daughter of Louis X. But it was still wise not to offend the powerful Duke of Burgundy any more than was absolutely necessary. They might be setting aside his niece from the succession, but they could not take the risk of labelling her a bastard into the bargain. And so was born the Salic Law: the nobles of France, headed by their new King Philip V, attributed their action to an ancient statute which absolutely forbad the throne of France to pass to a female. This nicely disposed of the problem of little Jeanne without causing too many difficulties with Burgundy, and to mollify the duke still further Jeanne was given in marriage to her cousin Philip of Evreux and the pair of them were invested with the tiny Pyreneean kingdom of Navarre, which had been transmitted to Louis X through his mother, who had been the only child of the last King of Navarre.

Unfortunately, however, this ingenious plan backfired, for both Philip V and his brother and successor, Charles IV, failed to produce a son. Each of them had three daughters; but the Salic Law declared that no woman could succeed to the throne of France. So, with the death of Charles IV in 1328, the direct male line of Philip the Fair became extinct. There was still, of course, Philip the Fair's daughter Isabella, wife of Edward II of England, who years before had been rumoured to have exposed the adultery of her sisters-in-law; but since she too was a woman, she was passed over, and the throne was given to her cousin Philip VI, whose father had been the brother of Philip the Fair.

Such an arrangement, however, proved far from pleasing to the son of Isabella, Edward III of England. He was little more than a child when his uncle died and the decision was made to bypass his mother and to offer the throne to Philip VI, but when he grew to manhood and had stabilized the uneasy domestic situation which he had inherited from the troubled reign of his father, he began to cast a considering eye on France. His mother had been the daughter of one of its Kings and the sister of three more; and therefore, Edward reasoned, she should have been the next heiress, and he was consequently the rightful King. If there had been doubts about whether the little Jeanne had really been the daughter of Louis X, there could be no doubt that he himself was the son of Isabella, and so there could be no doubt that his claim was legitimate. The Kings of England had always felt a strong interest in France: William the Conqueror had, after all, been Duke of Normandy before he became King of England, and the English Kings had owned not only Normandy but, through a marriage with the heiress of Aquitaine, large parts of southern France as well, until mismanagement and weak rule had enabled France to seize them back again. Now this claim of Edward's would give him a chance to recover what English Kings had always regarded as rightfully theirs; and going to war in a foreign country would also enable Edward to keep busy those restless nobles who had rebelled against his father and might perhaps in time rebel against him too.

16

So began the Hundred Years' War. It was not, contrary to its name, one hundred years of solid fighting. It was kept going intermittently, pursued with great eagerness by Edward himself and by his battling sons Edward the Black Prince and John of Gaunt, and then brought to a halt by Edward's francophile grandson and successor Richard II; it remained in abeyance during the reign of Henry IV, whose usurpation of the throne from Richard II had left him with more than enough to worry about at home, and it was then stirred up again with a vengeance by Henry IV's son, Henry V, who, as the heir of an usurper, needed to work hard to consolidate his position and knew well enough that one sure way of stopping his nobles from turning on him was to give them someone else to turn on. In this he was so successful that he was eventually given the hand of a French princess in marriage and accepted as heir to the French throne—the claim of the French King's own son being set aside—and shortly after Henry V's death in 1422 his baby son Henry VI was crowned King both of England and of France. In the early part of Henry VI's reign the struggle to achieve English domination of France was continued by the infant King's warlike uncles, but after that the internal troubles of the Wars of the Roses between the rival houses of York and Lancaster, which troubled England throughout the reigns of Henry VI and of his successors Edward IV and Richard III, brought the French wars to a halt and the English claim to France fell into abeyance.

It had a lasting effect, however. The English claim to France had been based on transmission through the female; and it so happened that the claim of the Yorkist side who were ultimately successful was also based on inheritance through the female line. Edward III of England, the King who had claimed the throne of France through his mother Isabella, had had seven sons. The eldest of these, Edward the Black Prince, had predeceased him, so when Edward III died in 1377 he was succeeded by his grandson, Richard II, only son of Edward the Black Prince. But in 1399 Richard II had been deposed and murdered by his cousin, Henry IV, whose claim to the throne was based on the fact that his father, John of Gaunt, had been the third son of Edward III. But there was still the second son, Lionel of Antwerp, to consider. His only child had been a daughter, Philippa. In France, of course, there could have been no question of Philippa or her descendants succeeding to the throne: she was a woman and, as such, debarred. But the Kings of England were claiming the throne of France precisely on the grounds that a woman *could* transmit the right to the throne: how, then—reasoned Philippa's descendants—could they possibly ignore the claims of Philippa? Should not her offspring have been the rightful heirs?

So at least it seemed to Richard, Duke of York, the great-grandson of Philippa. He was dissatisfied with the rule of his cousin King Henry VI. During the early part of King Henry's reign York could at least console himself with the reflection that, as the King's nearest male relative, he was the heir to the crown; but when King Henry married, all that changed, for now a son might be born to him who would displace York from the succession. York decided to act. From mute discontent he moved first to open warfare and then, gradually, to claiming that he, as great-grandson of Philippa, was the heir to the crown. York failed in his bid for the throne and was killed, but in 1461 his eldest son, Edward, was victorious at the Battle of Mortimer's Cross and succeeded in getting himself crowned as King Edward IV.

Thus England passed into the rule of a dynasty who claimed through the female line. The Yorkists fell from power twenty-four years later, when Edward IV's brother Richard III was killed by Henry Tudor at the Battle of Bosworth; but Henry Tudor's own claim to the throne was in turn based on the fact that his mother, Lady Margaret Beaufort, was the last surviving heiress of the Lancastrian claim to the throne. When Henry Tudor himself married the Yorkist heiress, Elizabeth of York, to ensure that his children could claim through both lines of descent, the importance of descent through the female line was still further underlined. In fact England's experience of female government had been far from happy: when the Empress Matilda had tried to succeed her father King Henry II after his death in 1135 the result had been civil war, for despite the fact that all the barons had sworn to her dead father that they would accept Matilda as his heir, they nevertheless preferred to see her cousin Stephen on the throne; and this was not the only example of disastrous rule by females that could be cited—Isabella of France and Margaret of Anjou had both earned for themselves the soubriquet of 'She-Wolf of France', the one by being party to the murder of her husband and the other by taking the government out of his hands, and Eleanor of Aquitaine in the twelfth century had found herself imprisoned by her husband when she had incited their sons to rebel against him. Despite all these unfortunate precedents, however, a series of dynastic coincidences had made it a well-established principle in England that the female could transmit and presumably, therefore, inherit the throne. In Scotland, too, the same principle was established: the Stuart Kings' claim to the crown came through the marriage of Robert the Bruce's daughter Marjorie to Walter the Steward, and for a brief period Scotland had even had a female ruler, Margaret, the Maid of Norway, until the little girl had died of seasickness on the long journey to her new kingdom from her birthplace in Norway.

The emphasis, however, was still very firmly on the transmission of kingdoms, rather than on the actual inheritance of them: a woman could act as a link in a dynastic chain, a bridge whereby rights could be transmitted from, say, grandfather to grandson, rather than be a candidate for power in her own right. Even the formidable Eleanor of Aquitaine, the twelfth-century heiress of the greater part of southern France, had had her options defined for her in almost purely dynastic terms: after her marriage to the French King, Louis VII, had failed to produce the necessary son, she found herself divorced. She had then to fend off at least one enterprising nobleman who thought that his quickest way to a fortune was to kidnap her and marry her by force, thus acquiring all her possessions, before finally becoming the wife of Henry II of England and spending the rest of her life fighting to ensure the inheritance of her younger children. To her husband, she was a traitor, because she encouraged their children to rebel against him; but in her own terms it could well be argued that she was merely ensuring the survival of her offspring. Similarly, the heiresses of the Crusader kingdom of Outremer

19

in the eleventh century, Jeanne, Queen of Navarre in the twelfth, and the co-heiresses Maria and Jadwiga of Hungary in the fourteenth were all nothing more than dynastic pawns to be married off as quickly as possible in the hope that they would produce sons; while when the English King Edward I finally succeeded in reducing to his obedience the north Welsh principality of Gwynedd, he was careful to capture Gwenllian, the baby daughter of its last prince, Llywelyn, and place her in a nunnery at Sempringham, where she could not transmit her royal blood.

This emphasis on women as transmitters of royalty rather than wielders of it remained true right up until the late fifteenth century. Isabella of Castile was Queen in her own right, but she nevertheless saw herself as secondary to her husband; her habit of referring to all decisions and actions as taken not by herself but by 'the King and Queen' led the Spanish chronicler Hernando del Pulgar to comment acidly that 'on such and such a day the King and Queen gave birth to a daughter'. Similarly, both Anne of Brittany and Mary of Burgundy, on finding themselves left as the young, orphan heiresses of the two most powerful duchies in Europe, made haste to throw themselves on the mercies of powerful husbands who could take care of them and their territories (as a matter of fact, both chose the same man—Maximilian of Austria— but Anne was forced by Charles VIII of France to break off her marriage with Maximilian and marry Charles himself instead).

There is one notable exception to this general pattern. In 1363 Christoffer, the only son of King Valdemar IV of Denmark, died. Valdemar had given Denmark the first strong rule it had known after decades of chaos, and in the twenty-three years of his reign he had earned for himself the nickname of 'Atterdag' ('again day'), after the long night of turmoil which had preceded his accession. The death of his son, however, posed a very serious threat to the security and stability which he had worked so hard to create. He did not even have any brothers, who could have provided him with nephews to whom he could have left his crown; but he did have two daughters. The younger of these, Ingeborg, was married to Heinrich of Mecklenburg, and had only a daughter, Maria; but the elder, Margrethe, was the wife of King Hakon VI of Norway, and seven years after the death of her brother, when she herself was still only 18, she gave birth to a son, Olof, heir to the thrones of both Denmark and Norway.

Five years later, in 1375, Valdemar died, and Olof succeeded him as King of Denmark. Since he was only 5 years old, however, he could not actually govern, and so his mother, Margrethe, was appointed his Regent. The fact that she herself was still only 23 years old does not seem to have troubled anyone, nor was it arranged that her husband should share in the regency with her—but then he was, after all, the King of another country, and might have been thought to be susceptible to divided loyalties. Margrethe governed Denmark for five years, continuing her father's policies, consolidating the power of the crown and maintaining the country's stability. Then in 1380, her husband, Hakon VI of Norway, died. Their son Olof was now King of both Denmark and Norway, but since he was still only 10 years old Norway too needed a Regent to govern for him, and once again the choice fell on Margrethe. At 28, she thus became the effective ruler of two countries

Her career did not stop there. The other Scandinavian kingdom, Sweden, was an elective rather than a strictly hereditary monarchy. It was currently being ruled by Albert of Mecklenburg, who had been elected King in 1364, but he was unpopular, and Margrethe's son Olof could lay a claim to the crown of Sweden through his paternal grandfather, Magnus Eriksson, who had ruled Sweden from 1319 to 1364. In 1386 the Swedish nobles came to an agreement with Margrethe that they would expel Albert of Mecklenburg and elect Olof as their King instead, but the next year, 1387, Olof died at the age of 17.

The death of Olof left both of his kingdoms of Denmark and Norway without a male heir, and Sweden without an acceptable replacement for Albert of Mecklenburg. The situation, however, does not seem to have created the alarm that might have been expected, because both Denmark and Norway turned at once to Margrethe. She had ruled both of them as Regent for Olof; she was already Queen Dowager of Norway, and now she was declared ruler of Denmark. Officially her position was to last only until a new King was chosen, but, despite her grief for the loss of her only child, Margrethe governed so satisfactorily that the Danish nobles did not bestir themselves to find anyone to replace her.

Margrethe herself, however, already had her successor in mind. Her only sister Ingeborg had married Heinrich of Mecklenburg and had had one child, a daughter, Maria, who had married Vartislaus of Pomerania. Maria's son, Erik of Pomerania, was thus Margrethe's great-nephew, and nearest male relative. In 1388 the nobles of Norway agreed to accept Erik as their King. It was an extraordinary decision, for Erik had in fact no blood relationship to any of their own royal line, but since he was still only 6 years old it brought no practical change, for Margrethe continued to govern as his Regent.

To install her nephew as King of Norway was a considerable achievement for Margrethe; but her greatest triumph was yet to come. The year after Erik's accession to the Norwegian throne, 1389, the Swedes finally rebelled against Albert of Mecklenburg and declared Margrethe 'first lady of Sweden and her lawful mistress', empowering her without qualification to bestow the crown of Sweden on whomever she chose. Albert of Mecklenburg still continued to resist, and it was not until 1396 that the Swedes succeeded in decisively defeating and imprisoning him. The next year both they and the nobles of Margrethe's native Denmark agreed to accept Erik of Pomerania as their King, and, now aged 14, he was crowned at Kalmar in Sweden, inaugurating what became known as the Kalmar Union of the three countries.

Margrethe had now nominally resigned power, but in fact she still continued to exercise it. In 1404 she slowly began to annex the crucially important duchy of Schleswig, one of the twin keys to Denmark's border, and by 1410, after waging a brief war, she had acquired for Denmark the strategically vital town of Flensborg. She had also succeeded in breaking the stringent conditions of government which had been enforced by the nobles when her son Olof had first succeeded to the crown, in recovering lands lost by her father and lands taken over by the powerful merchant guild of the Hansa, in winning for herself the support of the church and in curbing some of the ways in which peasants were abused by their masters. Her position was considerably strengthened by the fact that all three of the Scandinavian countries were under her control, meaning that none of them could ally with any foreign power against her, and also by the fact that she deliberately left vacant the two major offices of Steward and Marshal to avoid power passing out of her own hands. Although the Swedes were not completely happy with her rule, since they felt she relied too much on the advice of Germans and Danes, they never challenged her authority, and when she died in 1412, at the age of 59, she was the undisputed mistress of all the three kingdoms.

Margrethe's story is important for two reasons to any study of women and power before the sixteenth century: because it happened at all, and because, in Europe at least, it is unique. Anne de Beaujeu—referred to her by her father King Louis XI as 'the least stupid woman of my acquaintance'—had ruled as Regent of France for her brother King Charles VIII, but, although infinitely more astute and more capable than he, she had of course had to stand down when he reached his majority and enter political retirement. Margaret of York, an English princess who had married Duke Charles the Bold of Burgundy, had exercised considerable political influence in her adopted duchy, but in the end she had failed in her grand design of restoring Yorkist rule to England. There were similar restraints on the effectiveness of Caterina Sforza, the famous virago ruler who defended her two small northern Italian towns against besieging forces. Her children were taken hostage by her enemies; but, nothing deterred, Caterina appeared on the battlements of the town and, hoisting her skirts over her head to reveal the fact that she was pregnant, cried, 'Can't you see, you fools, that I am already making more?'—upon which her children, since they had not proved effective hostages, were released. But even such high-spirited defiance as this did not save Caterina from eventual defeat and imprisonment by Cesare Borgia, coupled, it seems, with the archetypal male revenge on the woman who dared to claim power, rape by her captor. Of the women rulers who preceded the sixteenth century, only Margrethe had truly held the fates of kingdoms in her hands. Her story provided the sixteenth century with a precedent for a woman exercising power superlatively well, but she stood alone.

Part I:

Wives of Kings

I

The Great Heiresses

THROUGHOUT the sixteenth century, there continued to
be women who attained the title of Queen in the traditional
way, by marriage with a King, and who spent their lives
exercising their traditional function of child-bearing. There
were some forty-eight women who, during the course of
the century, were consorts to European Kings. Their usual,
accepted recreations were needlework and religious devotion; they wielded no political power, and most made very
little mark on the history of their times. Their main value,
apart from as providers of children, was as transmitters of
land and property and as living representatives of diplomatic
alliances, and the extent to which it was the alliance rather
than the Queen herself who mattered was underlined by the
fact that if one Queen died, her widower might sometimes
take as his second wife her niece or sister. Thus Manoel
the Fortunate of Portugal married as his first wife Isabella,
daughter of the Spanish sovereigns Ferdinand and Isabella;
when she died, he married her sister Maria. By the time Maria
in turn died, the remaining two daughters of Ferdinand and
Isabella, Juana and Catalina, known after her marriage as
Katherine, were both married themselves and well past
child-bearing age, but, not deterred, Manoel took as his third
wife Juana's daughter, Eleanor of Austria, the niece of his
first two wives.

In the same way Katherine, the fourth daughter of Ferdinand
and Isabella, was married consecutively to two brothers, Prince
Arthur of England and his brother King Henry VIII; and
although Henry VIII was later to use this as an excuse to divorce
her, it did not seem to have troubled him during the first eighteen or so years of their marriage. It was only the combination
of Katherine's failure to produce a male heir and his own love

for another woman that prompted him to consider his marriage with his brother's widow unclean; at the time of their marriage it had been he who had taken the initiative. Nor would there have seemed anything particularly odd about such a marriage, since there had been precedents for it.

One of the most important of these precedents was still recent at the time of Henry VIII's marriage to Katherine of Aragon, and it is a story which is vividly illustrative of the rôles usually played by Queens who were, in their own right, heiresses. In France, towards the end of the fifteenth century, a crisis had arisen when the last Duke of Brittany, Francis II, had died without sons. He did, however, have two daughters; and since the Duchy of Brittany was more or less completely independent from France and the Salic law had never been introduced there, his elder daughter, Anne, was, from the age of 3, brought up as his heiress. In keeping with the new ideas of Humanist education that were beginning to filter through from Italy, she was taught French, Breton, Latin, Greek, and some Hebrew, making her exceptionally well educated for a girl of the period. Like so many states which shared a border, Brittany and its neighbour France were veteran enemies, and the Regent of France, Anne de Beaujeu, who was governing on behalf of her young brother Charles VIII, tried to use the fact that there was no male heir to the Duchy to destabilize the Breton government and, ultimately, to bring Brittany under the control of France. She persuaded some disaffected Breton lords to agree that unless Duke Francis produced a son, then Brittany would pass to the King of France. But the Breton Estates General decided that Anne of Brittany was able to succeed, so at the age of 10 she and her younger sister, who was next in line after Anne herself, swore a formal oath of good government, and Anne was crowned as Duchess in anticipation of her succession. Fathers who wished to ensure that the succession passed smoothly after their deaths had often had their sons crowned during their own lifetimes; now Francis II was applying the same principle to his daughter. It was a wise precaution, because two years later, in 1488, he was dead.

Although the new Duchess Anne was only 12 years old, she immediately by-passed the regency council, which was set up to advise her, and began to make her own decisions. But to fend off the schemes and ambitions of France she wanted help. Her father had betrothed her to the young English King Edward V, but after only a few months of rule he had been imprisoned and perhaps murdered by his uncle, Richard III. So Anne had to look elsewhere for a husband, and her choice fell on the heir to the Holy Roman Empire, the Archduke Maximilian of Austria.

Maximilian had already made one highly successful marriage. A few years before the death of Anne's own father, another powerful duke, Charles the Bold of Burgundy, had died without sons, and he too had been succeeded by a daughter, Mary of Burgundy, the greatest heiress in Europe. Charles the Bold had used Mary as one of the most important pawns in his diplomatic negotiations, and eighteen times he had promised her in marriage; but because he was never willing to commit himself and so lose her potential as a diplomatic counter, she was still unmarried at the time of his death. Finding it impossible to cope alone, she had immediately sent for Maximilian to marry her and take over the reins of government of her duchy. The marriage had been a personal as well as a political success, and the young couple had been very happy; but at the age of only 24 Mary had been fatally injured in a riding accident, leaving Maximilian a widower, with two young children, Philip (later to be called the Handsome), the new Duke of Burgundy, and a daughter, Margaret of Austria.

A marriage between Anne of Brittany and Maximilian of Austria held considerable advantages for both sides. Maximilian was a proven soldier with the considerable resources of the Holy Roman Empire to draw on, and would therefore prove invaluable to Anne in warding off French aggression; and she might, too, have taken into account the fact that he had proved an attentive and affectionate husband to Mary of Burgundy. Maximilian, for his part, had been finding Burgundy rather a handful to govern since the death of Mary; the inhabitants resented him as a foreigner, and had even gone so far as virtually to kidnap his young daughter, Margaret of Austria, and marry her to the King of France without her father's consent. He would not be sorry to leave

Burgundy behind and move on to Brittany, where he would be more welcome and would have a much freer hand.

The person not at all pleased by the prospect of such a marriage, however, was the Regent of France, Anne de Beaujeu. As the daughter of Louis XI of France, she had inherited her father's long distrust of both Burgundy and Brittany. King Louis had wanted to marry Mary of Burgundy to his own son, and had never forgiven Maximilian for forestalling him; now Anne de Beaujeu was determined to see that Maximilian did not pull off a similar *coup* to the disadvantage of France. Despite the fact that Anne of Brittany, in an attempt to safeguard her position, had already arranged for a proxy marriage to take place—with Maximilian's envoy pulling off his boot and stocking and inserting his naked leg into her bed in the traditional token that she was now Maximilian's wife—Anne de Beaujeu sent French troops into the Duchy. The Bretons were able to put up little resistance; Maximilian was too far away to be of any help; and the young Duchess found herself forced to agree to consider her betrothal to Maximilian dissolved, even though the papal dispensation releasing her from her contract to him did not arrive until a week after her second wedding, and to marry the young French King, Charles VIII, instead. The fact that Charles already had a wife—who, to complicate matters further, was Margaret of Austria, Maximilian's daughter by his first marriage to Mary of Burgundy—was merely a minor inconvenience: the marriage was declared dissolved, and the young Margaret, a divorcee at the age of 11, was sent home to her father Maximilian, who thus found himself simultaneously robbed of both bride and son-in-law.

The reason that Anne de Beaujeu had been so eager to arrange the marriage between her brother and Anne of Brittany was, of course, to ensure French control over the powerful Duchy of Brittany. This Celtic-speaking territory, fiercely independent, had been a thorn in the side of the Kings of France for far too long; now the death of its Duke without male heirs and the consequent succession of a very young girl presented the perfect opportunity, and with her usual political acumen Anne de Beaujeu—she who had been termed by her father 'the least stupid woman I know'—had not hesitated to exploit it. By the end of her regency, she was able to hand to her younger brother not only the territories their father had left him, but also control of the Duchy of Brittany. So successful had she been, indeed, that in the next century the chronicler Brantôme declared 'she governed so wisely and so virtuously that she was one of the great Kings of France.'

However, even within Brantôme's words of praise for her success lies the seed of her eventual failure. Brantôme had, for his time, rather liberal views on the subject of women—he was, for instance, a passionate admirer of the rakish Queen Marguerite of Navarre—but nevertheless he could think of no appropriate word to denote the concept, so alien to his times, of female authority, and had to fall back on describing Anne de Beaujeu as a 'King'. Her problem, however, was that she was of course not a King, but merely the eldest daughter of one. Although she was by far the most promising of the three surviving children of Louis XI—her sister, Jeanne, was deformed, and her brother Charles VIII was soon to involve himself in a series of disastrous and unwinnable wars in Italy—she nevertheless enjoyed only a brief period of power as Regent. As soon as her brother attained his minority, she retired from political life, while Charles VIII and his Queen, Anne of Brittany, took centre stage.

Despite his sister's acquisition of Brittany, the reign of Charles VIII was one of mixed fortunes. The same was true of his marriage. Despite the rather inauspicious start to their marriage, Charles and Anne of Brittany did appear to develop a genuine affection for each other, and lived together in peace and happiness, with Anne still being allowed to exercise power over her own duchy; but in the primary duty of a royal couple, the production of children, they failed dismally. Of the four sons born to them, none lived beyond the age of 4.

On the political front Charles suffered similar reverses. He had inherited an old claim to certain territories in Italy, and the internal troubles there soon led the Duke of Milan, Lodovico Sforza, to issue an invitation to the French to come and intervene. Charles seized his opportunity with alacrity, but no sooner had he crossed the Alps than the Italians, Sforza included, began to realize that in inviting outside interference they had made a disastrous mistake. Charles marched unopposed through Florence and down as far as the kingdom of Naples, to which he laid claim through the Anjou ancestors of his grandmother, but when he came to return to France it was a very different matter. He had to fight his way up the length of the peninsula, and returned from his expensive adventure with very little indeed in the way of concrete gains to show for it.

What he had acquired, however, was a considerable taste for the beauties and elegance of Italy. Queen Anne, who knew her husband well, had been afraid that he might prove susceptible to the charms of the south, and although she herself did not accompany him, she had ensured that only the ugliest women she could find went with the court on the journey. She had also written to him every single day that he was away. Her precautions had been in vain, though, because the Italians, hearing of the tastes of the King, had arranged that on his arrival at Asti he should be greeted by the eighty most beautiful women of the region—and Charles, who was very short, had duly stood on tip-toe to kiss every one of them. He returned from Italy with a book containing portraits of all the women he had slept with while in Naples, and also with an enduring fascination with more conventional products of the art of the Italian Renaissance. He brought home with him Italian artists and architects, and one of the places he was particularly anxious for them to work on was the Château of Amboise, where he had been born. He was so anxious to see it completed that he even had his masons working during the unpropitious season of winter, when they had to use fires to thaw the stone until it could be worked. His love of Amboise, however, was to prove unfortunate for him. One day he was walking through the château with Queen Anne, on his way to see a tennis match, when he suddenly caught his head a terrible blow against the low lintel of a door. The physicians were too frightened to move him and so, nine hours later, weltering in his own blood and lying partly in a passage which the courtiers had been accustomed to use for relieving themselves, he died where he had fallen. Anne, still only 22 and now a widow, was devastated by her loss and sobbed for two days on the floor of her chamber.

Because Charles VIII and Anne had failed to produce children, Charles's heir was his cousin, Louis, the Duke of Orléans. Charles VIII's father, King Louis XI, had distrusted the Orléans family, and had also been anxious to ensure that there was not a proliferation of princes of the blood who might cause problems to the King by demanding power, and so he had therefore married the Duke of Orléans to his own daughter, Jeanne. There were in fact rumours that his elder daughter Anne, later the Regent Anne de Beaujeu, was in love with Orléans; but Louis XI had chosen Jeanne as his wife instead. The reason for this had been that Jeanne was deformed, and therefore considered unlikely to be able to produce children: Louis XI was said to have remarked at the wedding that the progeny of the marriage would hardly cost much to keep, and the couple had indeed remained childless. But Louis XI's cunning plan to ensure the extermination of the Orléans line looked likely to backfire very seriously now that the Duke of Orléans had become the King of France, and was shackled to a wife who was unable to bear children. Fortunately, however, the Borgia Pope, Alexander VI, proved willing to grant a divorce if Louis would find a wife of suitable wealth and rank for Cesare Borgia, the Pope's illegitimate son. Cesare was duly married off to the wealthy Charlotte d'Albret and was created Duke of Valentinois, while Queen Jeanne was examined in the presence of twenty-seven witnesses and a finding was registered that the marriage between her and King Louis had never been consummated and was therefore invalid. Jeanne, who had never even been officially notified of the death of her brother and of her own consequent advancement to the crown, protested that even though she knew that she was not 'as beautiful or as well made as many other women', she nevertheless had lived with Louis as his wife and had had sexual relations with him. She backed down, however, when a particularly probing and embarrassing series of questions culminated in a request to undertake a physical examination of her to ascertain the nature and extent of her congenital deformity, to see if it incapacitated her either from sexual relations or from the bearing of children. Rather than submit to such an intimate examination, Jeanne accepted the verdict

33

of the court that she should be divorced, and at once retired to a convent, where the sanctity of her life was later to earn her canonization. So the Duke of Orléans, now King Louis XII, was a free man again, and able to take another wife. And his choice fell on the widow of his predecessor, the Duchess Anne of Brittany.

The marriage contract that had been drawn up between Anne and Charles VIII had stipulated that if there were no children of the marriage and Anne were to predecease her husband, then her Duchy of Brittany would pass to him and his heirs, ceasing to be independent and becoming instead a possession of the crown of France. If, however, it were to be Charles who died first—as had in fact happened—then Anne would have to marry the next King of France, thus ensuring that possession of her duchy could not pass outside the kingdom. That this was a very real possibility would have been very forcibly brought home to Louis by the fact that shortly after the death of Charles VIII Anne had in fact returned to Brittany, where she had very firmly taken up the reins of government and had begun to have coins struck bearing her image as Duchess. Louis XII had no desire to see this sort of sovereign state in existence on the borders of his own, and anyway, if court gossip was to be believed, he had been casting an interested eye on Anne ever since her marriage to Charles VIII. Thus, after a brief period of widowhood, Anne of Brittany became Queen of France for the second time, through her marriage with Louis XII.

Once again, a marriage which had started in rather unpromising circumstances actually turned out to be a perfectly amicable one. Louis allowed Anne a free hand in the running of her own duchy, and even sought her advice on the affairs of France. Their court was a brilliant one, frequented by poets, musicians and scholars, and marked by frequent elaborate festivals, and Anne even created an order of ladies, which she called 'la Cordelière', as a sort of equivalent to the male orders of chivalry. But once again Anne was to fail in her primary duty of producing a healthy male child: a son born five years after the marriage lived only a few hours. She did, however, give birth to two daughters—first Claude, and then Renée. This was of vital importance for France, because for her second marriage Anne, whose personal position was by now so much stronger than it had been when she was a beleaguered teenager with French troops overrunning her duchy, had been able to negotiate a marriage treaty that was much more favourable to Brittany than her first one had been. If she were to die childless, her husband Louis XII would rule the Duchy for the duration of his life, but after that it would revert to her own heirs. Brittany would therefore have become independent again, the very thing that three successive rulers of France had striven so hard to avoid. However, since Anne had daughters, and since she herself had provided a precedent for female succession to the Duchy, it would now pass to her elder daughter Claude.

That came about in January, 1514, when Anne, Duchess of Brittany in her own right and twice Queen of France, died, at the age of 38, probably of stones in the gall-bladder. She was buried at the royal French necropolis of St.-Denis, but, in token of her affection for her native duchy, her heart was removed and taken for separate burial in Nantes, then the capital of Brittany.

Two questions now became of vital importance: the marriage of Anne's elder daughter Claude, and the succession to the crown of France, and the two were intimately bound up together. Because Anne's husband Louis XII had had no children at all by his first wife Jeanne, and only two daughters by Anne herself, he had either to marry for a third time, in the hope of begetting a son, or face the prospect of the crown of France passing to his cousin Francis, Duke of Angoulême. This was a prospect that was not particularly pleasant to him. Louis himself had been a cautious King, with little time for the war-and-glory expeditions favoured by his predecessor, Anne of Brittany's first husband, Charles VIII; but Francis was young, gallant, and enthusiastic, and seemed only too likely to want to launch France on yet another series of costly and probably fruitless campaigns in Italy. Louis had watched Francis very carefully, and did not like what he saw. 'That big fellow', he said, 'will ruin everything.'

Nevertheless, Louis knew that a third marriage was by no means guaranteed to produce an heir, and he also had to consider the future of the Duchy of Brittany and of his daughter, Claude, who was now its Duchess. One obvious solution was to marry Claude to Francis of Angoulême, so that if he did indeed become King of France then Louis' daughter would be Queen and the Duchy of Brittany would once again be secured to the French crown. While Anne of Brittany had been alive she had always bitterly opposed this plan. She did not like Francis or his family, and perhaps she had never really accepted the principle that Brittany should be effectively annexed by the French crown; she was, after all, a Breton herself, and she had the interests of her duchy at heart. She had therefore tried to betroth Claude to the Archduke Charles. Louis, however, had disapproved of this. Either because he was afraid of his wife or because he did not wish to displease her, he took no public action, but he secretly annulled the contract and promised Claude instead to Francis of Angoulême. Now that Anne was dead, he was able to carry out that promise, and the wedding accordingly took place. The bride, Claude, cut a sorry figure: she was only 15 years old, was very small with a bad limp, and was still wearing mourning for her mother, for whom she cried throughout the ceremony. Nevertheless, she was now safely married, and Brittany, therefore, was linked once again to France.

Louis XII, however, was still not happy with the prospect of Francis of Angoulême as his successor, and therefore decided to take another wife, in the hope that, although he was now 52 and in poor health, he would be able to father a son who would displace Francis from the succession. His choice of a third bride fell on Mary Tudor, the sister of Henry VIII of England. The marriage was highly acceptable to the English King, who had recently discovered that his supposed ally the Archduke Charles had in fact been secretly negotiating with the French, and saw this as an ideal opportunity for revenge and for turning the tables on Charles. It was also greatly pleasing to Henry VIII's chief adviser, Cardinal Wolsey, since it was directly in line with the pro-French policy which the Cardinal liked to adopt whenever he could. The person it did not please, however, was Princess Mary herself.

Mary had in fact been betrothed since the age of 8 to the Archduke Charles, and this engagement had held out to her the promise of a glittering future, because a combination of advantageous marriages and premature deaths had brought Charles the richest inheritance of any ruler in Europe. His father, Philip the Handsome, had been the only son of the Austrian Archduke Maximilian, heir to the Holy Roman Empire, and of Mary of Burgundy. Through his grandfather Maximilian, Charles was an Archduke of Austria, and the only likely successor to his grandfather's title of Holy Roman Emperor; through his grandmother Mary of Burgundy, he received not only a claim to the French Duchy of Burgundy (which had in fact been confiscated by the French on the grounds that, as French territory, it was subject to Salic law and so could not be inherited by Mary or her descendants), but also, and more importantly, the Burgundian possessions of the Low Countries, consisting of the lands now known as Belgium and Holland.

In addition to this, Charles was also the heir of his mother, Juana, who as the eldest daughter of the Spanish monarchs Ferdinand and Isabella inherited from them not only Spain but also the Spanish possessions overseas, bringing her the fabled wealth of South America and the Indies. The succession to the Spanish lands was, however, complicated, for Ferdinand and Isabella had each ruled their respective kingdoms of Aragon and Castile quite separately, and the difficulty was worsened by the fact that their only son, Juan, had died young, leaving them only four daughters; and while Isabella's kingdom of Castile raised no objections to a female succession, Ferdinand's kingdom of Aragon had never had a woman ruler, and it was very uncertain whether or not it would accept one. So when Isabella died in 1504, and Juana and her husband Philip the Handsome succeeded to the throne of Castile, Ferdinand returned home to his own kingdom of Aragon and took a second wife, Germaine de Foix, in the hope of having by her a son who could prevent the succession crisis that might be precipitated if he were to die without a male heir. It was only because his marriage to Germaine proved childless that, on his death, the Spanish crowns were permanently united.

It was, however, not Juana who united them. In 1506, only

two years after the death of Isabella of Castile, Juana's husband, Philip the Handsome, died very suddenly, apparently after over-exerting himself playing the ball-game *pelota* and then immediately afterwards drinking too much cold spring water. Juana had been very much in love with her husband, so much so that she had often been driven to the point of despair by his frequent infidelities—she had once threatened one of his mistresses with a pair of scissors. Now, under the shock of her loss, her mind gave way completely. Refusing to believe that he was in fact dead, she would not allow his coffin to be buried or even covered up, and eventually she tried to kidnap it and ride away into the mountains with it, so that she could have her beloved husband always with her. At this point the Estates of the kingdom agreed with Juana's father Ferdinand that she was manifestly unfit to rule, and should be kept for her own safety under guard. So 'Juana la Loca'—Joanna the Mad—was incarcerated in the tower of Tordesillas, while her father Ferdinand ruled as Regent in her stead. And although Juana was not deprived of her title of Queen Regnant, it was understood that, in practice, once Ferdinand died it would be Juana's elder son, the Archduke Charles, who would reign as King in Castile as well as Aragon.

This, then, was the inheritance which the Archduke Charles claimed through his parents, and it was this formidable list of possessions—the Low Countries, Spain, America, and the prospect of the Holy Roman Empire—which had made the English King Henry VII so anxious to betroth his younger daughter Mary to Charles. A marriage ceremony had duly taken place in 1508, when Princess Mary was 12 and Charles himself was 8, and from then on Mary was known in England as 'the Princess of Castile'. Shortly before the death of Anne of Brittany, however, Mary's brother, who had now succeeded his father as King Henry VIII, made his momentous discovery that Charles, whom he had thought of as his ally, had been secretly negotiating with France, and in retaliation he broke off the match between Charles and Mary.

Mary herself was horrified at this turn of events, and was even more appalled when she learned that instead of the young and immensely wealthy Archduke of Austria, she

was now to be married to an ageing King of France. Dislike
of her prospective bridegroom, however, was not the only
reason for her unhappiness: it seems that she was already
conducting a secret love affair with one of her brother's
favourite courtiers, a handsome but rather stupid man by
the name of Charles Brandon. Brandon had already had a
distinctly chequered matrimonial history. He had contracted
one marriage, with a young girl in his guardianship, and
had had it declared invalid on a technicality; he had then
married a wealthy widow of twice his own age, run through
all her money, and then proceeded to have the annulment
of his first marriage declared invalid. He had therefore left
his second wife and returned to his first, who bore him
two daughters, but then died, enabling Brandon to consider
himself a free man again. None of this tangled web appears
to have deterred the Princess Mary, and the combination of
her love for Brandon, her disappointment at forfeiting her
title of Princess of Castile and her revulsion at the prospect
of marrying a man thirty-four years older than she was
reduced her to a terrible state. There were hysterical scenes,
and Mary even threatened suicide if forced to marry Louis.
Perhaps because she was Henry's favourite sister and, with
her striking, waist-length red-gold hair and beautiful blue
eyes, had been much petted by her parents, she expected
to get her own way. Henry, however, would not give in. He
told her that, although elderly, Louis was known to be a kind
man, and that if she would not submit voluntarily, he would
use force or have her put in the Tower.

But despite these threats, Henry was fond of his sister,
and had no wish to see her permanently unhappy. He was
also aware that the reports of Louis' health suggested that the
King might not live long. And so Henry and Mary seem to
have come, in secret, to an agreement: if she married this time
to please her brother and for the sake of a diplomatic alliance,
then in her next marriage she could marry to please herself.
Henry does not seem to have been in any doubt that her
choice would be Charles Brandon, but Brandon was a close
friend of his and Mary was his favourite sister and on this
occasion, at any rate, Henry was prepared to be indulgent.

So, somewhat mollified, Mary Tudor set off from England

to take up her new position as Queen of France, accompanied by an impressive suite of 400 lords, barons and knights, 200 gentlemen and eighty ladies (one of whom was Anne Boleyn, later to be the second wife of Mary's brother King Henry VIII). She had an atrocious crossing, after which she had to be carried unconscious through heavy surf to land. On her arrival she found her new husband to be every bit as bad as she had feared: 52 might have seemed old enough to a girl of 18, but Louis actually looked much older than his years. He had difficulty walking and breathing, and a sagging lower lip and his lack of teeth made him prone to constant dribbling. He was, however, as Henry VIII had promised her he would be, an attentive husband. One of his wedding presents to his new bride was the 'Mirror of Naples', an enormous diamond famous throughout Europe, as well as two huge rubies and a diamond and ruby necklace. Moreover, he had already exhibited to the court a huge assembly of rings, necklaces and bracelets which, he told them, he intended to let Mary have—but not all at once; each one would have to be purchased individually with kisses.

Mary, it seems, was content to pay the price. Indeed, she seems to have found marriage to Louis less of a trial than she had feared; even when he sent home the greater part of her English followers, after a brief period of tearful pleading for their return Mary suddenly discovered that in fact she enjoyed much more personal freedom without them. And when her beloved Charles Brandon was sent over by Henry VIII to thank Louis for his good treatment of Mary and to act as the English representative at her coronation as Queen of France, he had what must have been the rather disconcerting experience of being ushered into a chamber to find Mary and Louis in bed together, and behaving towards each other apparently with great affection and contentment.

Indeed, Mary was so complaisant to her husband that some shrewd observers at the French court suspected her of having an ulterior motive. The new Queen, it was reported, was deliberately trying to wear her husband out: court gossip was that 'the King of England has sent a hackney to the King of France to carry him soon and comfortably to Paradise'. Certainly after their wedding night Louis XII told his courtiers

40

that he had 'performed marvels', and whenever she could
Mary kept him up till late hours dancing and feasting.
Whether this was deliberate policy or not, the result came
quickly: on 1 January 1515, four months after the wedding,
Louis died.

Mary, now a widow and still only 18, did in fact seem to be
genuinely upset at the loss of her elderly husband. She had,
however, little time for any grief, for her own position was a
very delicate one. Court custom was that a widowed Queen
of France should clothe herself entirely in the traditional
white mourning costume, the 'deuil blanc', and retire into
complete seclusion for a period of forty days. At least part
of the reason for this was so that a close watch could be
kept on her to establish whether she was pregnant already
and, if she was not, to make sure that she could not become
so. This was seen as the most dangerous period, when a
lascivious widowed Queen could conceive a bastard whom
she could then attempt to palm off as the legitimate offspring
of the late King. The people most actively concerned to make
sure this did not happen were the heir-presumptive, Francis
of Angoulême, and his formidable mother, Louise of Savoy.
Louise had been waiting and planning for a long time now in
the hope that her adored son would become King; there still
exists a diary entry in which she records her jubilation that

> Anne [of Brittany], Queen of France, on the day of St. Agnes,
> 21st January, had a son; but he was unable to interfere with
> the exaltation of my Caesar because there was no life in him.

The woman who had thus rejoiced in Anne of Brittany's
dead child had no intention of being cheated now by any foul
play on the part of Mary Tudor. She and Francis maintained
a strict watch on the widowed queen to ensure that no child
of hers could prevent the ascension of Francis to the throne.

They watched her so closely, indeed, that Mary became
alarmed. Francis called on her daily—almost the only person
who, in the strictness of her mourning, was allowed to do
so. His ostensible purpose was to establish whether she were
pregnant or not, since, if Mary were to have a male child, the
boy would displace Francis himself from the succession. At
last he tired of dropping hints. He told her straight out that

his own wife was pregnant, and enquired whether she might be expecting a similar happiness. Mary told him that he was the only King in France, and Francis at once set about making plans for his coronation. His visits, however, did not cease. Moreover, he also dismissed all the attendants whom Mary had brought with her from England and substituted French servants who were instructed always to leave him and Mary alone together. Mary began to be very much aware of her own isolation and vulnerability.

Francis's intentions towards her have never been clear. At one stage, Mary herself seems to have thought that he might be intending to rape her; and it has been suggested that he might have been titillated by the fact that, despite Louis' vociferous noises about the consummation of the marriage, Mary still wore her hair in the loose, flowing style which usually indicated virginity. Certainly Mary Tudor was famed as one of the great beauties of the day, and Francis went to considerable pains to be alone with her. It was rumoured, however, that he was finally brought to his senses by his mother, Louise of Savoy, who pointed out to him the devastating fact that if he did rape Mary, then she might become pregnant—and bear a child who, if he were a boy, would then be able to supplant Francis himself in the succession. Perhaps this sobering reflection cooled his ardour; or perhaps he had, in fact, never been intending rape, for other rumours were that he had actually offered to divorce his recently married Queen Claude if Mary would marry him instead. To this, however, there were three very powerful objections. In the first place, since Claude was already pregnant Francis could not plead non-consummation of the marriage, and it would be difficult for him to find any other grounds for divorce which were likely to prove acceptable to the Pope; in the second place, the loss of Claude would mean the loss not only of Brittany, which three successive rulers of France had worked so hard to acquire and retain, but also of the territories left to Claude by her father Louis XII; and in the third place, Mary herself said no.

She seems, in fact, already to have made up her mind to rely on the half-promise she had extracted from her brother and on his known affection for her, and to marry Charles

Brandon, whom Henry had now created Duke of Suffolk. Brandon had already been over to France once since her marriage, sent by Henry to thank Louis for his kindness to Mary and to represent England at her coronation. Now Henry sent him back again, this time to be his representative at the funeral of Louis. Henry extracted an oath from Brandon, before he went, not to abuse his trust or show any partiality to Mary; but of course, if Henry had been really anxious to prevent this happening, he would not have sent Brandon as his representative in the first place but would have chosen somebody else. Given that he already knew of their affection for each other and had as good as promised Mary that her next husband should be of her own choice, it seems quite possible that by sending Brandon to Mary at this crucial time Henry in fact intended them to marry. He was, however, reluctant to avow this openly, since he was under pressure from his nobles at home. They wanted him to make use of Mary in another diplomatic alliance, and they would also inevitably be reluctant to see one of themselves, like Brandon, elevated above the rest of them through a marriage with the King's sister. Brandon was not even one of the old established nobility, but from a relatively new family. What would really suit Henry ideally was for him to appear to have had his hand forced in some way or other before he could give consent for a marriage between Mary and Brandon.

This was, in fact, what Mary's next move looked likely to precipitate. Whether Francis (now King Francis I) did indeed propose to her or not, she decided to confess to him her love for Brandon. Francis responded with the utmost gallantry; he would, he said, personally plead with Henry to allow this love-match. This was so convenient for Henry that some have been tempted to suspect his hand behind it: after all, if the English nobles were now to raise any objection to Brandon's advancement, Henry could reply that the marriage had the countenance of the King of France. As for Francis, the arrangement suited him too, since it took Mary off the international marriage market and meant that she could not now be used to cement an English–Spanish alliance—an alliance which would exclude France and be detrimental to her interests.

What happened next, however, was perhaps not quite so much in accordance with Henry's wishes. At the end of his first official audience with her, Mary asked Brandon to stay behind, alone. Then, weeping, she told him that if they went back to England without getting married first Henry might change his mind, or at any rate was liable to delay. According to the account he himself later gave to the King, Brandon tried to resist and to change her mind, but Mary would have none of it. Then, according to one version of the story, Francis I's mother, Louise of Savoy, suddenly entered the room, with an opportuneness which suggests deliberate design. Hearing of the couple's dilemma, she advised them to marry at once, and even told them of a priest who was just beginning mass in a private chapel of the Hôtel de Cluny. Mary and Brandon rushed off to find him, and were married within the hour.

The next morning Mary wrote to her brother King Henry VIII to confess to him what she had done. She begged for his pardon, and to make her appeals more persuasive, she tactfully enclosed a deed of gift making over to Henry all the considerable amount of jewellery that had been bestowed on her by her late husband King Louis. Brandon also added a letter of his own, pleading for the King's pardon and taking care to inform him at the same time that the marriage had been very thoroughly consummated and so could not be dissolved. Henry's reaction to all this is difficult to gauge. He certainly appeared to be angry; whether he actually was or not is difficult to say. He may have been secretly counting on just such an event taking place, or Mary may have been right in her estimation that his commitment to their marriage was only lukewarm and that he was quite likely to be diverted from it if his hand was not forced. At all events, after a two-month period of coldness Henry gave the newly married couple formal permission to return to England.

There they were greeted by the King in very friendly fashion. A second marriage ceremony was performed and celebrated with great festivities—for which, however, Brandon was asked to pay. Indeed, this was the case throughout their married lives: the price of their retention of Henry's favour was not only the gift to Henry of all Mary's French jewels, but also a heavy fine which was to place Brandon under an intolerable burden of debt, which he never managed to discharge. Nevertheless, Henry remained, for the most part, on good terms with them, and they settled down to a married life which seems to have been largely happy, although it was shadowed by Mary's poor health, by the early death of their only son, and by a quarrel which arose between them over the question of Henry VIII's divorce from Katherine of Aragon, when Mary took Katherine's side, and was consequently forbidden to come to court and threatened with prison, and Brandon took Henry's. Eventually, Mary's frequent illnesses (she seems to have suffered from porphyria, a disorder hereditary in the royal family) led to her death at the early age of 38. She left two daughters, Frances and Eleanor Brandon; the elder, Frances, was to become the mother of the three unhappy Grey sisters, Lady Jane, Lady Catherine and Lady Mary, while the younger, Eleanor, became Countess of Cumberland. Her only daughter, Margaret Clifford, married the Earl of Derby, and thus she too became, at least technically, a Queen, since the Earls of Derby were hereditary rulers of the Isle of Man, and thus bore the title of King of Man. The Derby family, too, found that the royal blood that Margaret Clifford had transmitted to them could be a curse as well as a blessing: her eldest son Ferdinando Stanley, Earl of Derby, attracted the attention of the Jesuits, who saw him as a possible successor to the crown if they were to succeed in their plan of assassinating Elizabeth I of England. They threatened him with death if he divulged the plan; but he did—and soon afterwards died. His death was widely rumoured to have been the result of poisoning by the Jesuits, whose plans he had betrayed, but he, too, may have been a victim of porphyria, inherited from his royal ancestors.

Six weeks after Mary's death, Charles Brandon married for a fourth time. This time his wife was his 14-year-old ward, Lady Katherine Willoughby. She bore him two sons, but both died in their teens, within half an hour of each other, of the dreaded sweating sickness, which had earlier killed his only son by Mary, Henry, Earl of Lincoln.

Mary Tudor's attitude to queenship seems to have been ambivalent. Before her marriage to Louis, she seems to have been almost equally attracted by marriage to Charles

Brandon, whom she loved, and by marriage to the Archduke Charles, who could make her mistress of half the known world. During the brief period when she was Louis' wife, many observers thought that she was doing her utmost to tire him out, and she certainly seemed willing to make up to her elderly husband in order to extract from him the copious amounts of jewels with which he plied her. But she was equally ready to hand over all those jewels to King Henry VIII if it enabled her to marry the man she loved; and although throughout her marriage to Brandon she always retained her title of 'Mary the French Queen', she very probably turned down a chance of retaining that title in reality by marrying Francis. It would not have been unthinkable for her to do so—Anne of Brittany had married two Kings of France in succession, and one of them had divorced his first wife for her—but Mary chose Brandon instead, and never seems to have regretted that decision until the day she died.

One of the results of Mary's choice was, of course, that Francis I's wife Claude, daughter of Louis XII and Anne of Brittany, remained Queen of France. In personal terms, Claude would have been no rival for Mary: she was very small, she had a pronounced limp and she certainly had nothing like the striking good looks of the English princess, though the Italian ambassador did comment that her 'grace of speech' was sufficient compensation for her lack of beauty. Having been married to Francis in tears, she had been abandoned immediately after the ceremony by her bridegroom, who promptly returned to his current mistress. It was only the urgings of his mother, Louise of Savoy, which persuaded Francis that he could not afford to neglect his bride and his chances of producing an heir; so, after a three-month absence, he returned to Claude at her favourite Château of Blois. Even her ensuing pregnancy did not, however, serve to cement the marriage; it did not prevent the growth of rumours that Francis intended to divorce Claude and marry Mary Tudor instead, and even after Mary had returned to England as the bride of Brandon, Claude was not, as had been the custom, crowned Queen of France at the same time as her husband was crowned King. Although she was the daughter of the last King of France and Duchess of Brittany in her own right, she had to wait for that honour until, after three years of marriage, she gave birth to her first son, the Dauphin Francis.

Francis also used the birth of his son to enable him to carry out what both of his two predecessors had failed to do: he made permanent the link between France and Brittany which had existed for two generations in the persons of Anne of Brittany and her daughter Claude. The Dauphin Francis was, as his own eldest son, heir to the kingdom of France and, as Claude's eldest son, heir also to the Duchy of Brittany. Claude drew up a will naming the Dauphin as her heir, and now Brittany could never again be an independent power and a challenge to French authority.

The will was to come into effect sooner than might have been anticipated. Admirably fulfilling the primary duty of a sixteenth-century Queen, Claude had produced seven children in seven years, four girls—Louise, Charlotte, Madeleine and Marguerite—and three boys, Francis, Henry and Charles; but she was always delicate, and her incessant pregnancies took a severe toll on her health. Finally, in 1524, she died, after an outbreak of boils had failed to receive proper treatment. She was only 25 years old.

She had been, said the chronicler Brantôme later in the century, 'very good and very charitable and very gentle to everyone, and she never did any injury to anyone in her court or in her kingdom'. Her main love had been the gardens of her favourite Château of Blois. Her husband Francis I had paid her little attention while she was alive, but after her death he seems suddenly to have realized what he had lost. If his own life, he declared, could buy her back, it was a price he would not hesitate to pay, for he would never have thought that the severing of the marriage-bond would cause such a wrench.

His feelings could only have been confirmed by his second marriage. Since Claude had left him such a large family, there might not have seemed to be any immediate need for him to marry again; but many of the children had inherited their mother's precarious state of health, and in the event only Henry and Marguerite were to live to their full maturity. Francis would certainly be glad of more children to leave the succession absolutely secure. That was one reason for marrying; but another, and much more pressing one, was that effectively, he had no choice. For whereas Francis's first marriage had been contracted largely to secure an inheritance, the Duchy of Brittany, his second one was to be a political necessity, to seal a vital alliance.

II

Seals of Alliances

LOUIS XII had been right in his estimation that Francis would wish to emulate Charles VIII by launching a campaign in Italy. The Angoulême branch of the Valois family, to which Francis belonged, had an old claim to the Duchy of Milan, through the fact that an ancestress of theirs, Valentina Visconti, had been the only legitimate survivor of the Visconti dukes who had once ruled Milan. The Visconti had been rather unsavoury and unpopular rulers: the last duke, Filippo Maria, was an immensely stout and horrifically ugly man who had refused to have his portrait painted, could not stand up without the assistance of a page, liked rolling naked in his garden, had a special room built in his palace for hiding from the thunder in, had had his first wife executed after discovering her in the same room as a page, and had refused to consummate his marriage to his second wife after he had heard a dog howling on their wedding night. The direct result of this latter eccentricity was, of course, that he had no legitimate children; but he did have an illegitimate daughter, Bianca, who had married the successful soldier of fortune Francesco Sforza, and when Filippo Maria died, Sforza seized the duchy in the right of his wife. Perhaps because the people had tired of Visconti rule, or perhaps because Sforza was a just and energetic ruler, his usurpation had been a successful one, and Milan had since remained in the hands of the Sforza family. But although Filippo Maria had not had any legitimate children, he did have a sister, Valentina. Valentina had shared in the rather sinister reputation of the Visconti family: it was alleged that it was witchcraft practised by her which had been responsible for the insanity of her brother-in-law, the French King Charles VI, and when her husband, Louis Duke of Orléans, was murdered in a Paris street, his right hand was cut off to incapacitate his corpse from performing the sort of black magic of which the bodies of wizards were supposed to be capable. Nevertheless, there was no denying that Valentina did have a legitimate claim to the Duchy of Milan.

Louis XII had been the grandson of Valentina, and thus heir to her rights, and he had duly invaded the Duchy, expelling its Duke, Lodovico Sforza, and claiming it for his own. But to capture a city was one thing; to keep it was another. Although Duke Lodovico died in a French prison, his two young sons had been taken to the safety of the Emperor Maximilian's court at Innsbruck, where they lived until 1512 when the Swiss, whose territories bordered the Milanese lands, decided to intervene. They were at odds with the French and this was hampering their profitable trade with Milan. So in exchange for being granted the Milanese towns of Lugano and Locarno, they ousted the French troops and installed Massimiliano Sforza, elder son of Duke Lodovico, as Duke of Milan.

They had reckoned without Francis I. He too was descended from Valentina Visconti, and in 1515 he declared his intention to reclaim the Duchy. This need to reclaim Milan had, in fact, provided Francis with a splendid opportunity. The courts of Europe were steeped in the Arthurian legends and tales of chivalry, with their glorious knights and stirring descriptions of battles; moreover, the ideal of the Renaissance man, which was beginning to make its influence felt, demanded that a Renaissance king should be not only a scholar, a sportsman, a huntsman, a musician and a statesman, but should acquire military glory. This last could be difficult to achieve—the quest for it was to involve Henry VIII in some very expensive and unsuccessful European campaigns—but it seemed that here Francis had a golden opportunity. The young Massimiliano Sforza was a far cry from his famous grandfather, Francesco, who had won Milan through force of arms; he was a nervous and barely educated young man, hardly able to read or write, who was said never to have been seen to laugh and was considered highly unlikely ever to have been able to regain his duchy if he had not been helped by the Swiss. Francis could therefore judge his prospects of success to be good, and the rewards would certainly be worth having: not only the fame and glory of the conquest, but also control of Milan, which would constitute a direct blow at the dangerously increasing might of the Habsburg empire.

There was already sufficient power concentrated in Habsburg hands to worry France; but the one ray of hope was that the many different territories which the young Habsburg heir, Charles, stood to inherit were geographically scattered and would therefore be difficult to rule as a united bloc of lands. It was while trying to acquire territory which would join his lands in France with those in the Low Countries that the last Valois Duke of Burgundy, Charles the Bold, had been killed in battle; his death had cut short his plans before they had been brought to fruition, and now his great-grandson faced the same problem. The Burgundian Low Countries, which he had inherited from his father, were uncomfortably far away from Castile, which had come to him from his mother, and from Aragon, which would pass to him on the death of his grandfather; and between them lay France, traditional enemy of both Burgundy and Aragon. Since the direct overland passage from Spain to the Low Countries ran through such hostile country, journeys from one to the other had to be conducted by sea, and this was not without its inconveniences. Storms and shipwrecks were a constant danger: Charles's parents Philip and Juana, on the way from the Low Countries to Castile, had been forced ashore in England, and although the English King Henry VII had treated them with great honour, they had, nevertheless, been very much aware that they were effectively in his power, which had led Philip to sign a trading treaty so favourable to English mercantile interests that his own Flemish merchants had christened it the 'Intercursus malum', the 'cursed treaty'. Similarly, at an earlier period when Charles's grandparents Ferdinand and Isabella had sent their daughter Katherine, Juana's sister, to marry Arthur, heir to the throne of England, her voyage had been delayed for months by contrary winds, and her sister-in-law, Charles's aunt Margaret of Austria, had fared even worse. On her way from Spain to become the wife of Ferdinand and Isabella's only son, Juan, who was already her husband by proxy, she was first of all driven ashore at Southampton in a rowing boat, and then found herself caught in such violent gales in the Bay of Biscay that, believing she was bound to be shipwrecked, she tied to her hand a purse containing gold pieces (so that whoever found her body could pay for her burial) and an epitaph that she had written for herself:

> Cy-gist Margot, la gentille damoiselle,
> Qu'ha deux marys et encore est pucelle.

Translated, this reads 'Here lies Margot, the noble young lady, who has two husbands and is still a virgin'—referring to the fact that her first husband, Charles VIII of France, had divorced her while she was still a child in order to marry Anne of Brittany, and that she now appeared likely to die before she could reach her second husband.

In fact, no member of the royal family ever had died on the dangerous voyage, but that still did not make it any more desirable that the only way for Charles to get from one part of his domains to another was via such an unreliable and potentially unpleasant journey. There was, however, a possible alternative, which, although a much less direct route, did offer certain other advantages. This was to travel through northern Italy. Charles's grandfather on his father's side was the Emperor Maximilian of Austria, and Maximilian had his chief seat at Innsbruck, not so far from the Italian border. After the death of his first wife, Mary of Burgundy, and the failure of his attempts to marry Anne of Brittany, Maximilian had taken as his second wife Bianca Maria Sforza, the niece of Duke Lodovico of Milan, and he maintained close contacts with the Milanese court; indeed, the current Duke, Massimiliano, owed his unusual name to the intervention of Emperor Maximilian, who had taken such a fancy to the boy that his name, which had originally been Ercole, had been altered in deference to the Emperor. Maximilian had consolidated his Milanese interests still further by giving refuge to Massimiliano and his younger brother Francesco when their father Duke Lodovico had been driven out of his duchy by Louis XII of France. The two boys had been brought up first at the court of Innsbruck by Maximilian and his wife Bianca Maria Sforza, who was their first cousin, and then had been sent to the court of Maximilian's daughter, Margaret of Austria, in the Netherlands. This had completed the process

52

of bringing them thoroughly into the Habsburg orbit, and they had grown up, it was said, with markedly German habits of thought and with a very high regard for Emperor Maximilian. Now that the Swiss had installed the elder of them as Duke, therefore, Maximilian, and by extension his grandson and heir Charles, had a very useful ally. The Duchy of Milan was practically at their disposal, providing them not only with a possible land route for travel between the disparate parts of the Habsburg empire, but also with a very useful base for interfering in the domestic politics of Italy. Already the Spanish controlled the kingdom of Naples, which made up the southern part of the Italian peninsula; now northern Italy, too, was poised to fall under their influence. Francis's march on Milan was an attempt to counteract this uncomfortable build-up of power.

The Swiss enjoyed the reputation of being some of the most fearsome soldiers in Europe, and it was they who had finally brought down Duke Charles the Bold of Burgundy; seasoned warrior though he was, he had found it impossible to deal with Swiss troops fighting on their own difficult terrain. Francis, however, took the Swiss by surprise by crossing the Alps by a previously untried route, and then succeeded in defeating the Swiss army at the battle of Marignano. He rounded off his triumphant incursion into Italy by meeting Leonardo da Vinci, who for some years now had been court artist to the Sforzas, and by persuading the great painter to return to France with him. Massimiliano Sforza proved quite happy to do likewise; he resigned his duchy and took up residence in France in exchange for a pension from Francis which would keep him in comfort.

The campaign had been a triumph for Francis; but he, too, was to discover that it was easier to conquer a duchy in a foreign country than to keep it. On 1 January 1519 the Emperor Maximilian died. His grandson Charles automatically inherited all the lands which were Maximilian's by hereditary right, but the succession to the Empire was, at least in name, elective, not hereditary, and the death of Maximilian therefore precipitated a bitter struggle for the prestigious title of Holy Roman Emperor, which was mainly carried on by vigorous bribing of the Electors, the various temporal and spiritual potentates whose votes determined the succession to the Empire. There were three main candidates: Henry VIII of England; Francis I of France, claiming in his right as Duke of Milan; and Charles, the late Emperor Maximilian's grandson, who since the death of his other grandfather Ferdinand of Aragon had been Charles I of Aragon and Castile. Of these, however, only Francis and Charles could be counted as serious contenders. Henry VIII simply did not bribe with sufficient energy; perhaps he under-estimated the venality of the Electors, or perhaps for him the stakes were less high. For Francis and Charles, however, this was far from the case. Both took the question of the succession to the Empire very seriously indeed. If Charles were to be successful, France would be completely encircled by dominions controlled by him; if Francis were the victor, then he would be in a position to drive a very damaging wedge straight between the two blocks of lands already controlled by Charles.

The contest, however, was an unequal one, for Charles was able to draw on the fantastic resources of the banking house of the Fuggers of Augsburg. The spending power made available to him by loans from the Fuggers far outmatched anything at Francis's disposal, and so Francis found himself systematically outbid in his attempts to secure the votes of the Electors, and the title of Holy Roman Emperor therefore went to Charles. Being the fifth Emperor of that name, he thus became not only Charles I of Spain, but also the Emperor Charles V.

This would have been humiliation enough for Francis to swallow, but worse was to come. In 1521, two years after his election to the Empire, Charles V decided to bring Milan once more into his own sphere of influence. Massimiliano Sforza was still living in France on his French pension, and therefore could not be reinstalled as Duke; but he had a younger brother, Francesco, and since Massimiliano had resigned his title to the Duchy Francesco could be put forward instead. The French who had been left behind to garrison the city were defeated by the famous mercenary Giovanni delle Bande Nere (Giovanni of the Black Bands), whose mother Caterina had been the illegitimate daughter of Duke Galeazzo Maria Sforza of Milan and was thus the half-sister of Bianca Maria, the second wife of Charles's grandfather the Emperor Maximilian. Francesco Sforza was therefore installed as Duke, and the next year, at the battle of La Bicoque, he defeated the French army which had been sent to expel him from the city—a defeat which was personally as well as politically difficult for Francis I since the French commander, Lautrec, was the brother of Francis's current mistress.

Determined to recapture the strategically vital Duchy, and stung by the failure of his army, Francis decided to go to Milan in person, in the hope of imitating the glorious exploit of nine years before when he had succeeded in taking the Duchy. To assist him he took with him the relics of St. Louis, the crusading thirteenth-century King of France. Whether thanks to the relics or not, Francis did indeed recapture Milan. But almost immediately afterwards, in a battle at Pavia with the troops of the Emperor, the French were disastrously defeated, and Francis himself was taken prisoner.

This was a blow of catastrophic proportions. Quite apart from the extreme personal humiliation it entailed for Francis, it also meant that he was personally and politically in the Emperor's power, and he was well aware that the terms which Charles would propose for his release were hardly likely to be generous. Fortunately, the government of France was being ably directed by his mother, Louise of Savoy; but that was the only redeeming feature of an otherwise calamitous situation. To make matters worse, shortly after his arrival in Madrid, where his captors had taken him so that he could negotiate with the Emperor for his release, Francis fell very seriously ill, and for a while hovered on the verge of death. It is possible that he had, in fact, little wish to live; certainly his death would have solved one of France's problems, since he himself constituted the Emperor's principal weapon and by dying he would deprive his enemies of their trump card. Slowly, however, he began to recover, under the care of his devoted sister, Marguerite of Navarre, who had been sent to him by their mother Louise of Savoy to nurse him, since Louise herself was occupied in governing her son's country during his absence.

Recovery brought with it its own problems. The Emperor Charles was very clear on what he wanted in exchange for giving Francis his freedom: those French territories which had once formed part of the old Duchy of Burgundy, to which he laid claim through his grandmother, Mary of Burgundy, but which had been withheld from her by the French crown on the grounds that, since they were French, they could not be inherited by a woman. Mary's father, Duke Charles the Bold, had been a considerable thorn in the side of the French King of the day, who had been only too delighted to be able to use this excuse to dismantle the overmighty Burgundian state; and the last thing Francis wanted was to see the resurrection of the Duchy which had once posed such a threat to France. In a dramatic bid to reduce his own value as a hostage, he declared that rather than surrender the French lands which had once formed part of the Duchy, he would abdicate and order that his eldest son, the Dauphin Francis, should be crowned in his stead. The Emperor Charles would thus be robbed of the pleasure of holding the French King as his prisoner; he would find himself in possession of nothing more than an ex-King, and he would therefore be deprived of his only bargaining counter.

This would, however, be a desperate step, and one that Francis would prefer to take only in the case of absolute necessity, so he also made other plans, which might come to fruition in the event that he did not, in fact, have to abdicate. His primary need was for allies, who could help him combat the dangerously growing power of the Emperor, and in this he was fortunate, because international opinion, which had previously been very much against him, had swung back in his favour. Before his defeat at Pavia, he had been surrounded by enemies: Henry VIII of England, whose wife Katherine of Aragon was the Emperor's aunt, the Pope, Clement VII, and the powerful city-state of Venice had all been so alarmed by French territorial ambitions that they had allied with Charles V in an anti-French coalition which was intended ultimately to achieve the virtual dismemberment of France, which would be shared out amongst them. Charles would take the Burgundian lands which had for so long been denied him; and Henry VIII hoped to reassert the old English claims to Normandy and to the Duchy of Aquitaine, which had passed to the English throne by inheritance in the eleventh and twelfth centuries respectively but had long since been conquered by the French. Henry might even be able to lay claim to the throne of France itself, which had been promised to the English King Henry V in the right of his wife Katherine, Henry VIII's great-grandmother, as a result of which the Kings of England had ever since had themselves proclaimed as Kings of France at their coronations.

These grand plans, however, were not to be realized. Gradually it was borne in on the Emperor's allies that the defeat and imprisonment of Francis had not in fact brought their own hopes any nearer to fulfilment, and that there were, indeed, worrying signs that without the French presence to act as a counterbalance to his power, the Emperor was now growing dangerously strong and would, if he chose to, soon be able to turn on his former allies. The anti-French coalition therefore began to drift very rapidly apart, and to accelerate its dissolution Francis's mother Louise of Savoy, in her capacity as Regent of France during his absence, sent a messenger to England to propose an alliance between the two countries which would be cemented by a marriage between Francis and the 10-year-old Princess Mary Tudor, only child of King Henry VIII and niece of the Mary Tudor who had married Louis XII of France and with whom Francis himself had once contemplated matrimony.

The Emperor Charles, however, had no intention of letting any such marriage take place. He knew very well indeed what a desirable matrimonial catch the young Princess Mary of England was: in the first place, she was his cousin—his mother Juana had been the sister of Mary's mother Katherine of Aragon—and in the second place he had until very recently been betrothed to Mary himself. The great attraction of marriage with her was that since she was the only legitimate child of Henry VIII and her mother, Katherine of Aragon, was by now almost certainly too old to produce more children, Mary was in effect the heiress of England, and whoever married her could ultimately expect to succeed to the English crown. For Charles, however, this advantage had eventually been outweighed by her youth—at 25, he was impatient to marry and produce an heir as soon as he could, and he would have to wait some years before Mary was nubile—and by the vast dowry of the bride he eventually chose, Isabella of Portugal. But although he had decided not to marry Mary himself, he had no wish to see Francis to do so and thus step into the position of heir to England. Henry VIII, who had been greatly offended by Charles's rejection of his daughter in favour of Isabella of Portugal, and who was beginning to be seriously mistrustful of Charles's good faith, was very ready to embrace the French alliance; but Charles still held the master card. Francis was, after all, his prisoner, and Charles also possessed one sure method of preventing him from marrying Mary Tudor—marrying him to someone else.

Moreover, Charles had the ideal candidate to hand. The Habsburg ruling house of Austria, to which Charles's father Philip the Fair had belonged, had taken as its motto 'Bella gerant alii: tu, felix Austria, nube' ('Let others make war: you, happy Austria, marry'), and although Philip the Fair had died before the age of 30, he had nevertheless managed to leave behind him seven children, two boys and five girls. Charles V therefore had five sisters, who could be used in matrimonial alliances, and the eldest of these, Eleanor of Austria, would, he felt, make a very suitable bride for Francis.

Eleanor had already been married once: at the age of 20, she had become the third wife of King Manoel the Fortunate of Portugal, who was thirty years older than she was and had already been married in succession to two of Eleanor's own aunts, the Infantas Isabella and Maria, sisters of Eleanor's mother Juana. Two years after the marriage, however, Manoel had died, and Eleanor had now returned to her brother's court in Spain. Charles had already made one further attempt to use her to cement a diplomatic alliance, when he betrothed her to the Constable of Bourbon, a French nobleman who had quarrelled with Francis I about the inheritance of his wife (the daughter of the former Regent of France, Anne de Beaujeu) and had therefore fled from France to transfer his services to the Emperor Charles, who had made use of him in his campaigns against the French in Italy. But although Bourbon had in fact made a major contribution to the capture of Francis, and had been promised both

Eleanor and the Duchy of Milan in exchange for his services, Charles could not now afford to honour those promises. He needed Eleanor for a more important purpose: to prevent the marriage of Francis to Mary Tudor.

Powerless to do anything else, Francis agreed to this marriage. He went further: he agreed to abandon his claim to the Duchy of Milan, and, most momentous of all, to cede to Charles the disputed inheritance of Burgundy. He had apparently conceded everything he had ever fought for. Furthermore, he agreed that, in exchange for his own release and for permission to return to his kingdom, his two sons, the Dauphin Francis and Henry, Duke of Orléans, should go to Spain as hostages in his place, to guarantee the fulfilment of the treaty. The exchange took place on an island in a river marking the border between France and Spain, and after a year's captivity, Francis was able to return to France.

There he immediately set about doing whatever he could to repudiate the ignominious treaty which he had been forced to sign. As a first stage, and to secure himself allies against Spain, he moved to cement the marriage with Mary Tudor, and early the next year his betrothal to her was actually celebrated at Greenwich. The marriage was vigorously encouraged by Henry VIII's chief advisor, Cardinal Wolsey, who had not forgiven Charles V for breaking a promise made that Wolsey should be the next pope, and who was very anxious that his generally pro-French policy should not be disrupted by a marriage between Francis and Eleanor of Austria. Not everyone, however, was as anxious as Wolsey was for the Princess Mary to be betrothed to Francis. Mary's mother Katherine of Aragon, as the aunt of the Emperor Charles, was naturally anxious not to see her daughter contracting a marriage which went against Charles's plans, and the citizens of London, accustomed to regarding Spain as a traditional ally and France as the traditional enemy, were greatly hostile to the prospect of a French King becoming the husband of the heiress of England. There was, moreover, the question of the two French princes who were being held hostage in Spain. So even while the marriage of Francis and Mary was apparently being determined, an escape clause was inserted into the contract. The Princess Mary was to marry either Francis himself, or, failing him, his second son, Henry, Duke of Orléans, who was currently a prisoner in Spain with his elder brother the Dauphin Francis.

Almost as soon as this treaty had been signed the political situation in Europe was violently transformed by the news of a most startling event. The Emperor's troops, under the leadership of the French rebel the Duke of Bourbon, were still in Italy. As was so often the case with sixteenth-century armies, their pay had fallen well into arrears, with the result that they were extremely disaffected; and Bourbon himself, who had abandoned his estates in France and now found that his promised reward of marriage with the Emperor's sister Eleanor had failed to materialize, had nowhere to go and seemed now to have nothing left to lose. Close at hand, however, was a city which contained easily enough wealth to keep the army loyal—Rome itself. In desperation he attacked it.

Bourbon himself was killed during the first assault on the city, but his troops, now leaderless, fought on. They easily overwhelmed the defences and, with no one to restrain them, launched what came to be known as the Sack of Rome. Monks were killed, nuns raped; the Pope himself was forced to take refuge in the castle of St. Angelo, where he found himself in a state of siege. Christians throughout Europe were shocked at such a violation of the Holy City by the army of a Catholic Emperor, and the strength of feeling against Charles was reinforced by two additional factors. In the first place, the Pope at once dispatched messengers calling on all Christian princes to give him assistance against the Emperor; but also, and much more importantly, Charles's fellow-rulers immediately realized that despite the obloquy the action of his troops had brought upon him, it had in fact also succeeded in increasing yet further his already dangerously growing power, since it meant that the Pope was effectively a prisoner in his hands, and would therefore be unable to do anything that would displease him.

Anxious to bolster his own position against this overmighty enemy, Francis once again asserted his alliance with England, though this time it was definitely his son Henry Duke of Orléans, rather than himself, who was to marry Mary Tudor.

Before any such marriage could take place, however, young Henry would have to be released from the Spanish prison where he and his elder brother had been languishing ever since they had been sent to Madrid in exchange for their father's release. Francis's concern for his sons can only have been exacerbated by the reports he heard about the conditions of their confinement: the two princes, neither of them yet in their teens, were kept in a single dark room which had only two stools, a pallet, and bars on the window; they had nothing to do, only a dog as a companion, and during the two years that they had been in captivity not only had their education been completely neglected but they had even forgotten their own native language of French. Even Henry VIII of England had been touched by their plight, and had offered to give the Emperor Charles the famous fleur-de-lys jewel which had once belonged to the Emperor's grandfather Maximilian if only Charles would release the boys.

But although Henry VIII's attempt at mediation had not been effective, there was someone else who possessed rather more influence over Charles, if only she could be persuaded to exercise it: his aunt, Margaret of Austria, who was currently acting as Regent of the Netherlands for him. Margaret of Austria had had an unhappy personal life: first she had been divorced by the French King Charles VIII so that he could marry Anne of Brittany, then her second husband, Juan of Spain, had died five months after their marriage, while the child which Margaret was carrying at the time of his death was born prematurely and did not live. Margaret had, however, found great happiness in her third marriage to Philibert the Fair of Savoy, and although Philibert too had died very young, she treasured his memory and that of the period she had spent in his Duchy of Savoy. Fortunately for Francis, his mother, Louise of Savoy, was Philibert's sister, and therefore she was able to appeal to Margaret of Austria, on the basis of this connection, to ask Charles to alleviate the treatment of the two little French princes.

So successful was Margaret's intervention in this respect that a further possibility began to emerge. Somehow or other, peace would have to be made between Francis and Charles;

and who better to act as negotiators than the aunt of one and the mother of the other?

So a meeting was arranged at the city of Cambrai, conveniently situated for Louise to reach from the French court and Margaret from her Flemish domains, and peace was finally concluded between France and Spain, a peace which, in honour of the two negotiators, was known as the Ladies' Peace. By its terms, the two princes were to return home to France the following year, and with them was to come Charles's sister Eleanor of Austria to be Francis's second wife. So in March 1530 France received both its returning heirs, and also its new Queen.

A marriage arranged under such circumstances could perhaps hardly be expected to be a happy one. Certainly to the two little princes, the sister of the man who had kept them in prison for so long must have seemed like the worst of all possible stepmothers; and there were rumours that Francis, too, was less than enamoured of the marriage, and that he had in fact been deliberately postponing it at the request of his imperious mistress, Anne d'Heilly, Madame de Pisseleu. Certainly Madame de Pisseleu accompanied him when he attended Eleanor's coronation, which did not seem to bode well, and soon there were rumours that the King had developed a personal dislike for the Queen, and could not bring himself to sleep with her—rumours which spread as the marriage remained childless. The fault does not seem to have lain with Eleanor's appearance—her portraits show her to be attractive, despite the jutting lower lip which her grandmother, Mary of Burgundy, had transmitted to all the Habsburgs, and she was widely agreed to be an elegant woman who was termed an 'ornament to the festivals of the court'—but nevertheless she failed utterly to attract her husband, perhaps because he was already so very much taken up with his various mistresses. And, thwarted on the personal front, Eleanor was equally unsuccessful in carving out any kind of political career for herself; not only was there already her powerful mother-in-law, Louise of Savoy, architect of the Ladies' Peace, active at court, but there was also Francis's sister, Marguerite of Navarre, who was a writer in her own right and an influential dispenser of patronage. There was, quite simply, nothing for Eleanor to do. Her marriage, which had made her a central feature of European diplomacy for so long, had, now that it had actually taken place, reduced her to a nonentity.

In the absence of any rôle to play, she passed her time in travelling round the kingdom, showing herself especially fond of the southernmost parts, which lay the nearest to her native Spain. Her journeyings continued when, after sixteen years of loveless marriage, she found herself widowed for the second time by the death of Francis I. If there had been little enough place for her as Queen Consort, her rôle as Queen Dowager was non-existent: ten years later, a French commentator on his country's affairs was to write:

> . . . there is no people less exposed to the government of women, since the law of the Salians, that is to say the law of the French, excludes them from succession to the kingdom . . . on the death of their husbands Queens are almost completely degraded in rank so that they do not retain even a shadow of the dignity of Queen.

Thus robbed of any effective reason for her existence, Eleanor of Austria returned to the Netherlands, where she had lived as a child and where her sister Mary of Hungary was now acting as Governor in succession to their aunt Margaret of Austria, and then went finally to Spain, where she lived a lonely life until she died, at the age of 60, in 1558—the same year as her brother the Emperor Charles and their sister Mary of Hungary, and only three years after the death of their mother, the unhappy Juana the Mad.

The next two Queens of France were, however, to go a considerable way towards disproving the view that a French Queen was necessarily a political nonentity. Francis I's elder son, the Dauphin Francis, had predeceased his father, and so it was the younger son, Henry Duke of Orléans, who succeeded Francis as Henry II. The young duke's betrothal to Mary Tudor had long since been broken off, and he had instead been married to Catherine de' Medici, a scion of the wealthy banking family who had, for 150 years, been the effective rulers of Florence, and niece of the Medici pope Clement VII. Catherine's mercantile ancestry and lack of royal blood made this an extremely unusual marriage for a member of the French royal house, and indeed at the time it was arranged Henry was still only Duke of Orléans, not heir to the throne, so it was never envisaged that Catherine would be Queen of France. Fate, however, had decided otherwise, and had placed her on the throne.

It was not a well-omened marriage. Bride and groom were both only 14, and both had had trying childhoods. Henry had only recently returned from his long and distressing captivity in Spain; Catherine, whose parents had both died before she was two months old, had been brought up by her uncle, Pope Clement VII, during the difficult period when he was effectively a prisoner of the Emperor Charles V. In theory the young husband and wife should have had this common dislike of the Emperor Charles to draw them together, but any unifying effect this might have had was very much out-weighed by the fact that Henry was already deeply attached to the mistress who was going to command his whole-hearted devotion for the rest of his life, Diane de Poitiers. Francis I had personally intervened to bring about the liaison; disturbed at his son's withdrawn state on his return from his Spanish captivity, he had asked Diane to 'civilise' him. This she did with triumphant success, and although she was nineteen years older than the young prince, she never lost her hold over him. Moreover, Catherine herself was plain, with eyes that bulged and a lower lip that stuck out, and she was also a big eater with a plump figure, which was to increase in bulk throughout her life. She made a poor contrast to Diane, whose elegant body, toned by cold baths and a strict exercise regime, was to provide the model for sculptors and artists.

Three years after the marriage of Henry and Catherine, Henry's elder brother, the Dauphin Francis, died suddenly and mysteriously. The young prince was only 18, and this fact, coupled with the shortness of his final illness, meant that, as so often in the sixteenth century, poison was immediately suspected as the cause of his death. His cupbearer was arrested, condemned of his murder, and sentenced to death by being torn apart by horses. Rumour, however, was by no means satisfied of the justice of this verdict. It was, after all, notorious that the home of the art of poisoning was

Italy—Caterina Sforza, who had married into the Medici family, had instructions for slow poisoning in her book of beauty care—and Catherine was, moreover, the daughter of the man to whom the notorious Machiavelli had dedicated his book *The Prince*, and disciples of Machiavelli were certainly not going to stick at political assassination. It is now possible, given knowledge of the medical history of the young Dauphin's family, to suggest that he died of natural causes, as a victim of the hereditary condition porphyria, but such knowledge was unavailable in the sixteenth century, and popular opinion did not hesitate to speculate that Catherine de' Medici had poisoned him, in order that her husband should thereby succeed to the throne and she should become Queen of France.

This rumour could perhaps have drawn force from the fact that Catherine herself seemed relatively unsurprised by her sudden elevation from Duchess of Orléans to Dauphine. That was, however, because it had been prophesied to her. Catherine had already begun to take a very considerable interest in the popular sixteenth-century study of astrology, and was a lavish patroness of astrologers, including the celebrated Nostradamus. By them she had already been confidently assured that she would be Queen of France.

Another of the astrologers' predictions, however, seemed less likely to be fulfilled. Catherine would, she was told, become the mother of ten children, all of whom would wear crowns; but for the first ten years of her marriage she did not succeed in producing even one, and her position therefore became an extremely difficult one. Although she was popular with her father-in-law, who appreciated her Italianate sophistication, her interest in culture and intellectual developments, and her understanding of the Italian architecture which he was so anxious to encourage in France, her husband was completely engrossed in Diane de Poitiers; he had little use for his wife at the best of times, and if she was unable to provide him with an heir, he might well have no use for her at all. Her uncle, Pope Clement VII, who could have protected her, had died the year after her marriage, and the new Pope would have no particular reason for refusing Henry permission to divorce her.

Then she was rescued. At first it had, as usual, been assumed that her failure to conceive must be her own fault, and to save herself the shame of being divorced she had even offered to go voluntarily into a convent. But it was gradually realized that her husband in fact suffered from a congenital malformation which was preventing him from fathering a child. Like his successor Louis XVI when faced with the same dilemma two centuries later, Henry was at first reluctant to submit himself to a surgeon, but soon had to accept that this was his only way of obtaining an heir. As soon as he had done so, Catherine, after ten years of childless marriage, at once became pregnant, and proceeded to fulfil her astrologers' predictions by producing ten children in all—although only five of them were to grow up to wear the crowns which the astrologers had promised them. Even as a mother, however, she was not able to triumph over her husband's mistress Diane de Poitiers, who, to Catherine's chagrin, was promptly put in charge of the royal children's education.

Catherine's ten pregnancies, and her constant attempts to see as much of her children as she could despite Diane de Poitiers' guardianship of them, kept her fully occupied during the years that followed, so that she remained very much in the background even when her father-in-law Francis died, making her Queen, and she played no part in the major political decisions of the early part of the reign. Diane de Poitiers reigned supreme: it was her initials and portraits that decorated the luxurious new châteaux which were being built and furnished for the court, and it was in large measure to suit her political convenience that when a bride was being sought for the little Dauphin, Catherine and Henry's eldest son, the choice fell upon the little Mary, Queen of Scots, whose mother Mary of Guise was a member of the powerful Guise family who had allied themselves with Diane. Diane, now Duchess of Valentinois, reigned as effective Queen of France, while Catherine, not of royal blood and almost permanently pregnant, had no influence at all. She had no part to play in her husband's decision to declare war on Spain, which was prompted by his lasting hatred for the country where he had been kept in confinement as a child, nor did she have any say when, defeated by the Emperor Charles's son and successor Philip II, Henry was forced to make a peace which was to be cemented by marriages between Henry's sister, Marguerite of France, and the Duke of Savoy, and between Elisabeth of France, Henry and Catherine's eldest daughter, and Philip II himself. She was, however, naturally present at the festivities that were held to mark this double betrothal, and she thus became an eye-witness of the event that was to change her life.

Catherine's favourite astrologer, Nostradamus, had fore-told that the lion would be killed in its golden cage. The phrasing was so obscure that it was not a prediction which meant very much to anybody—until Catherine's husband Henry II appeared at the tournament to celebrate this double wedding of his sister and his daughter in a fine golden hel-met, and was struck in the eye with a spear by the captain of his Scots Guard. He lingered in agony for ten days, and then died.

Catherine was now no longer wife of the King of France, but mother of the King instead—a much more tenuous position, and one which was very poorly defined. In the thir-teenth century, Blanche of Castile had exercised the Regency of France for her son, St. Louis, and much more recently Louise of Savoy had done the same when her son Francis I was held captive in Spain. But matters were much less clearcut now because the new King, Henry and Catherine's eldest son Francis, was 16 years old—young enough to be very heavily influenced, but not young enough for it to be necessary to institute an official Regency. In the event, Catherine found herself able to achieve scarcely greater pol-itical power than she had exercised under her husband. She managed to take a personal revenge by exiling Diane de Poitiers from the court and extracting from her the Chateau of Chambord and the crown jewels, both of which had come into her hands during the reign of Henry II; but when it came to political decisions, she found herself having to give way to her daughter-in-law, the new Queen of France: Mary, Queen of Scots.

Mary had been Queen of Scotland from her cradle, follow-ing the death of her father King James V, and at the age of 5 she had been brought to France to be brought up there as

the future wife of the Dauphin. The reasons for choosing her
as the next Queen of France had been twofold. In the first
place, there was a long tradition of friendship between France
and Scotland: the fact that both were traditional enemies of
England had formed a common bond between them which
had come to be known as the Auld Alliance. A King of
France who found himself at war with England would call
upon the King of Scotland to distract the English by attacking
them along their northern border, and the Kings of Scotland
would similarly receive French aid if they were campaigning
against their powerful neighbours. It was as a result of this
policy that Henry II employed the Scots Guard whose captain
had accidentally killed him, and also as a result of it that
Mary's father, James V, had married two French princesses in
succession: first Madeleine, daughter of Francis I, who had,
as her father feared she would, succumbed to consumption
in the cold Scottish climate after less than a year of marriage,
and then Mary of Guise, who had borne him Mary, Queen
of Scots. It was this French mother who provided the second
reason for the choice of Mary, Queen of Scots, as a wife for
the Dauphin, since the powerful Guise clan, and their ally
Diane de Poitiers, were very anxious that the next Queen of
France should be well-disposed towards them, and with this
in mind had powerfully urged to the King the advantages of
acquiring a daughter-in-law who would bring his son not
only the title of King Consort of Scotland, but also a claim to
the throne of England itself, since in Catholic eyes Elizabeth
Tudor was illegitimate and Mary, Queen of Scots, was therefore the rightful heir to the throne. So Mary had been chosen
and, given the political and religious instability of her native
Scotland, she had been brought to France, where she could
be educated in a manner that befitted the future Queen of the
country.

There Mary, a pretty and clever child, had charmed the
whole court, and had delighted her Guise relatives by the
ease with which she was able to enchant not only her husband the Dauphin Francis, a sickly child who warmed to her
energy, but also her father-in-law the King and her husband's
younger brother, the little Prince Charles, as well. The one
person who was not obviously enraptured by Mary was her

mother-in-law, Catherine de' Medici: Mary, who along with the royal children had been brought up in the care of Diane de Poitiers, made no secret of the fact that she despised the mercantile history of the Medici family, and this led to a cold-ness between the two women. As a result, Catherine knew that while Mary was in the ascendant, and her Guise uncles had the ear of the young King Francis II, there would be little chance for her to exercise power. Her exclusion, though, was not to last long. In December 1560, Francis II, still only 17 years old and King for a mere eighteen months, died of an abscess in his ear.

His young wife, Mary, Queen of Scots, was now a widow. Like an earlier Mary, and like Anne of Brittany in the previ-ous century, she might well have been offered the chance of becoming Queen of France for the second time: her young brother-in-law, who had now succeeded as King Charles IX, had always been fond of her, and seems to have entertained thoughts of asking her to marry him. His mother Catherine de' Medici, however, was having none of that. She had never liked Mary, and she was certainly not going to see her become her daughter-in-law for the second time. Perhaps in revenge for the remarks about her descent from a family of bankers, she also intervened to prevent a proposed marriage between Mary and the heir to the throne of Spain, Philip II's son Don Carlos—though here she unwittingly did Mary a favour, since Don Carlos's always precarious state of health would within a few years degenerate into outright madness. So Mary was forced to return to Scotland, and her Guise uncles to accept, for the moment, a political back seat, while Catherine de' Medici took up the regency on behalf of her son Charles IX.

Although Charles had not been allowed to marry Mary, a Queen he nevertheless had to have, and the choice in due course fell on Elisabeth of Austria. Catherine, who had had so much to put up with on account of her own ancestry, had chosen a daughter-in-law whose descent was beyond reproach: her father, the Emperor Maximilian II, was the nephew of the Emperor Charles V, and her mother Maria was Charles V's daughter. This marriage between cousins had been deliberate policy, as part of an attempt to ensure that the two branches of the Habsburg family, which were now based in Austria and Spain, did not grow apart, and in accordance with this intention Elisabeth's sister, Anna, had recently become the fourth wife of Philip II of Spain, who, as her mother's brother, was her own uncle. Philip II's third wife had been Catherine de' Medici's daughter, Elisabeth of France. Catherine, who was a great believer in diplomatic marriages as a cementer of alliances, had found it useful to have the King of Spain as a son-in-law, and now that the death of her daughter Elisabeth had severed the connection, this marriage between her son and Philip's sister-in-law offered a convenient way of re-establishing a family link between France and her powerful neighbour Spain. Moreover, both the Austrian and the Spanish branches of the Habsburg family were supporters of the Catholic church against Protestant reform, and there was beginning to be disturbing evidence in France of rapidly growing numbers of converts to the views of the Geneva-based reformer John Calvin. Catherine's own son, King Charles IX, was proving willing to listen to Admiral Coligny, who was one of the leaders of the reforming party in France, known as the Huguenots, and Catherine, the niece of a Pope, might well have hoped that the irreproachably Catholic Elisabeth of Austria at her son's side would provide a useful counterbalance to what she saw as the disturbing influence of Coligny.

Certainly the 16-year-old Elisabeth proved, on her arrival in France in 1570, to be every bit as personally pious as Catherine could have hoped. She was also an attractive girl, with blonde hair and dark eyes. However, like so many foreign Queens arriving in a new country, she soon found that her claim to her husband was to be disputed by an already well-established mistress. Charles IX, who at 20 was four years older than his bride, was in some ways a sensitive young man, of marked artistic tastes, but he was also a highly-strung and sickly youth, suspicious and given to violence. In his wilder moments he had been known to kill and torture small animals with his bare hands, and his anger could turn against people, too. Apart from Coligny, the only person who seemed to be close to him was his mistress,

Marie Touchet, the beautiful young daughter of a magistrate, by whom he had already had a son and who was, moreover, a Huguenot. Not only was Elisabeth unable to attract her husband away from her rival; unlike her great-aunt and predecessor, Francis I's second wife Eleanor of Austria, she also fitted in poorly with the lavish dances and festivals of the Valois court. Despite the absence of sympathy between her and her husband, Eleanor of Austria had at least been acknowledged as ornament to the court festivities; but her great-niece Elisabeth, speaking only German and accustomed to spending a part of every night in prayer, found herself very much out of place amongst the elaborate courtly entertainments.

She was also deeply troubled to find herself in a court which was prepared to tolerate Huguenots. Her sister-in-law, Marguerite of Navarre, reported that when Coligny came to kiss her hand she blushed bright red, shrank back and would not allow him to touch her. Instead of being able to moderate her husband's policy, as her mother-in-law Catherine de' Medici seems to have hoped she would, her own temperament and the poor relations between her and her husband combined to exclude her completely from political life. After her husband had finally been panicked, by being told of threats to his life and throne, into ordering the mass killing of Huguenots which became known as the St. Bartholomew's Day Massacre, Elisabeth knew so little of what was going on that, when told of the deaths, she actually asked if her husband was aware of them; when informed that he was, and that they had actually been carried out at his express command, she could only say, 'My God, pardon him.'

Elisabeth did at least fulfil one of the duties of a sixteenth-century Queen, by becoming pregnant; but when the baby was born, it was a girl, who by the Salic Law could not succeed to the throne of France. The child was given the name of Marie-Isabelle and was sent by her grandmother Catherine de' Medici to Blois, where she would be safe from the political turmoil which was agitating the capital in the wake of the massacre of the Huguenots. No further pregnancy followed, and two years after the birth of Marie-Isabelle, when Elisabeth was still only 20, her husband

71

Charles IX, whose health had never been good, began to show unmistakable signs of approaching death. His symptoms appeared to be those of tuberculosis; he also suffered from terrifying nightmares and hallucinations, mainly about the St. Bartholomew's Day Massacre which had been such a blemish on his reign, and it has been suggested that he made his condition worse by continuing to indulge in his favourite pastime, hunting, and over-vigorously blowing his hunting-horn. He died in May 1574, at the age of 24, leaving Elisabeth a widow after only four years of marriage.

She stayed in France for two years more, as young royal widows sometimes did (Margaret of Austria, after the death of her young husband Juan of Spain, had remained for two years with her bereaved parents-in-law). Then, in 1576, she returned to her native Vienna. The little Marie-Isabelle was left in France, where two years later, at the age of 6, she died. When Elisabeth returned to Austria, still only 22 and obviously fertile, her family at once began to make plans to contract a second dynastic marriage for her; but Elisabeth refused point-blank. Certainly her first experience of matrimony had scarcely been encouraging enough to make her wish to attempt it at a second time, but the reason she gave was a religious one, since the Catholic church had declared that while second marriages were to be allowed on sufferance, it was preferable for a widow or widower to remain single. Any possibility of a second marriage for her receded still further when she dedicated herself to the Third Order of St. Francis; she had a convent built close to the Imperial palace in Vienna, and although she herself did not actually take the veil, she spent her time from then on in charitable works and in religious contemplation until her early death at the age of 38. The only distraction from this life of piety was the continued financial support which she provided, from her own considerable resources, for her sister-in-law Marguerite of Navarre, sister of Charles IX, who had alienated her own family by her disregard for convention and by her succession of lovers. Elisabeth provided Marguerite with an annual income—the sole reminder in her later years of her time as Queen of France, and a strange link between one of the most pious of sixteenth-century Queens and one of the most notorious.

Charles IX's successor as King of France was his younger brother, Henry III. Henry had always been Catherine de' Medici's favourite child, and in pursuance of the fulfilment of Nostradamus's prediction that all her children would wear crowns, she had contributed to the engineering of his election as King of Poland, one of the few countries where the crown was conferred not by heredity but by vote. It was on his way to take up his new crown, in the year before his elder brother's death, that Henry, escorted by his mother, had made a stop at Nancy, capital of the Duchy of Lorraine where his sister, Claude, was Duchess, and had just given birth to a child. Catherine and Henry stayed for the celebrations that were held to celebrate the baby's baptism, and it was there that Henry met Louise de Vaudémont, who was a cousin of his brother-in-law the Duke of Lorraine. Louise was young, quiet and pious, with pretty blonde hair; Henry, by contrast, was brilliant, flamboyant, and known to be sexually attracted to men as well as women. Nevertheless, perhaps because Louise's looks were similar to those of Marie of Clèves, whom Henry loved but who was the wife of the Prince de Condé, he amazed the entourage who accompanied him by falling immediately and openly in love with Louise, and following her everywhere until his departure for Poland after three days of festivity.

That, at first, appeared to be the end of the matter. But Henry had been in Poland only a few months when his brother, Charles IX, died, making him King of France. The Polish nobles were proving difficult to manage, and Henry was only too delighted to have the opportunity to return to a very much more attractive and more powerful kingdom. Slipping out of the country to avoid any attempt to force him to stay in Poland, he went first to Italy, where he passed some months in leading a life of luxury and pleasure, marred only by the fact that he seems to have caught there a venereal disease which may have rendered him incapable of fathering children. Then he returned to France, only to learn that his first love Marie of Clèves had died in childbed—poisoned, said the rumour-mongers, by Henry's mother Catherine de'

Medici out of jealousy at Henry's attachment to her, but in all probability of perfectly natural causes. His grief was great: he took to prayer and to conducting himself like a penitent, and he also announced his intention of taking a wife, Louise de Vaudémont, whom he had seen for only three days the year before, but whose looks were reminiscent of Marie's, and whose kinship to the powerful Catholic family of Guise-Lorraine might bring Henry some useful political allies.

Louise thus became Queen of France. She was never crowned, and she took no part at all in political affairs, which were still very much the province of her mother-in-law, Catherine de' Medici, but she was, nevertheless, very much the pet and the favourite of her husband, who treated her rather like a living doll. Henry had by this time surrounded himself with a circle of favourites, known as the king's *mignons* ('sweethearts'), young men who were, like Henry himself, flamboyantly effeminate and who delighted in dressing up and decking themselves in jewels, often putting on women's clothes and encouraging the ladies of the court to dress in male attire. Henry therefore took a great interest in Louise's wardrobe, and would spend hours dressing her, doing her hair, and taking her with him on his lengthy travels in search of new animals for his menagerie (he was particularly fond of dogs). When not occupied in this way, or when Henry was with his *mignons*, Louise, like her predecessor Elisabeth of Austria, busied herself with religious devotion.

She had a lot to pray for. In the first place, her marriage, not greatly to anyone's surprise, remained childless, which meant that, after the death of her husband's younger brother, the heir to the throne became Henry's brother-in-law, Henry of Navarre. Navarre was a Huguenot, and would therefore be completely unacceptable to the powerful Guise family, who had been close to the throne ever since their niece Mary, Queen of Scots, had been briefly Queen of France, and were also related to Louise herself. France had seen its first War of Religion in 1562; now, with the prospect of the accession of Henry of Navarre if the marriage of Henry III and Louise remained childless, the situation deteriorated sharply. Faced with the antagonism to him of the powerful Catholic League, headed by the Guises, which had forced him out of Paris and driven him and Louise to take refuge in Blois, Henry III's response was to order the assassination of the Duke of Guise. Eight months later there was another assassination—but this time the victim was Henry III himself, stabbed to death by a Dominican monk acting to avenge the Duke of Guise and to punish Henry for what the Catholic party saw as his manifold iniquities.

Louise was genuinely grief-stricken at the loss of her husband. She went into deep mourning, first at Chenonceaux, and then, even further away from the court, in a convent at Moulins, where she devoted herself to fasting and prayer until her death at 48.

III

The Political Queen

THE piety of both Elisabeth of Austria and Louise de Lorraine-
Vaudémont was in stark contrast to the scandalous lifestyle
of their successor as Queen of France, Marguerite of Navarre.
Marguerite's marriage, like theirs, had been intended primarily
as the seal of an alliance, but unlike Elisabeth and Louise,
Marguerite was not content to sit on the sidelines of the political
world. She lived through one of the most dramatic and eventful
periods in France's history, and she was an active participant
in some of the most important political events of the time. Her
career is an interesting example of the Queen who, rather than
merely functioning as a political symbol, played a more central
rôle.

Marguerite was the daughter of Henry II of France and
of Catherine de' Medici, and after the death of her father,
in accordance with her mother's policy of using dynastic
marriages to cement diplomatic alliances, and also because
of Catherine's desire to see fulfilled Nostradamus's prediction that all her children would wear crowns, several royal
husbands were proposed for her from a very early age. When
she was 10 years old, her mother had offered her as a wife for
the heir of Spain, Don Carlos, primarily with the intention
of ensuring that her much-disliked daughter-in-law Mary,
Queen of Scots, would not marry Don Carlos instead; then
the King of Hungary was suggested, and, when Catherine's
elder daughter Elisabeth de Valois, who was married to
Philip II of Spain, died, Catherine proposed that Marguerite
should take her sister's place and become Philip's fourth
wife, thus ensuring the continuation of a family connection
between the ruling houses of France and Spain. When this
was secured instead by the marriage of Catherine's son
Charles IX to Philip's niece Elisabeth of Austria, Catherine

decided to use Marguerite in her most daring matrimonial plan of all—as a wife for the young Henry of Bourbon, heir to the tiny kingdom of Navarre on the borders of France and Spain.

The connection between the royal families of France and of Navarre went back two generations, to the marriage between Marguerite, Duchess of Alençon, widowed sister of Francis I of France, and Henry d'Albret, King of Navarre. Their only child, a daughter named Jeanne, had been given in marriage by her cousin, King Henry II, to Anthony of Bourbon, who as a descendant of the youngest son of St. Louis would be next in line for the throne if the Valois line should die out. It was to prove a politically momentous marriage, for by 1560 both Anthony and Jeanne had been converted by the teachings of the reformer John Calvin, and became leading members of the Huguenot community. They had also had two children, a son Henry and a daughter Catherine, and they, too, had been brought up in the reformed religion. It was distinctly uncomfortable for Catherine de' Medici, who was acting as Regent for her son Charles IX, to have Huguenots so near the throne, but preferring, as usual, to settle differences by matrimonial alliances rather than by hostilities, she proposed a marriage between the young Henry of Navarre and her own daughter Marguerite of France. He would, after all, be King of Navarre on his mother's death, and Catherine was probably influenced too by the prediction made by her trusted astrologer Nostradamus that Henry of Navarre would one day be King of France. This was a prediction that came one step closer to fulfilment when his father, Anthony of Bourbon, was fatally wounded during an engagement in the Wars of Religion, leaving Henry as the next heir to the throne after Catherine's own sons.

Ever anxious to avoid conflict, Catherine managed to remain on negotiating terms with Jeanne d'Albret even after the latter had joined forces with her brother-in-law the Prince de Condé and had taken up arms in the Huguenot cause, and she continued to press on with plans for the marriage despite opposition from Philip II of Spain, who wanted Marguerite to marry King Sebastian of Portugal, from the Pope, who was refusing to grant a dispensation and even sent a legate to the French court to forbid the marriage, and from Jeanne herself, who despised Catherine for her mercantile ancestry. Jeanne also disliked her future daughter-in-law, who she said wore too much make-up and had her corsets laced too tightly, and she declared that the Valois court as a whole was 'the most vicious and corrupt atmosphere imaginable'; she was shocked, she said, to see men who wore jewellery and to hear stories of women who made advances to men, and she hoped that her son, whom she had brought up so carefully in the much stricter ways of Calvinism, would never have to live there. She herself certainly wanted to be away from the court as soon as possible; she asserted that holes had been drilled in the walls of her room to enable people to spy on what she was doing, and said that she was being made ill as a result of the difficulties and tensions of the marriage negotiations.

Her stay at court was certainly to be cut short, though not in the way that she had hoped. Her vague complaints of ill-health suddenly gave way to a serious illness; four days later she was dead. She was only 44, and, as always in cases of sudden death in the sixteenth century, rumour immediately declared her to have been poisoned by a pair of perfumed gloves sent to her by Catherine de' Medici, since it was popularly believed that Italians were experts in the art of poison. Modern medical opinion has suggested that she might in fact have been killed by a combination of tuberculosis and an abscess in her right breast, and it does seem unlikely that Catherine would have wanted to kill her when she had, in the past, gone to considerable lengths to stay on the best terms possible with her. However, the rumours spread apace, and when Henry, now King of Navarre since his mother's death, arrived at Paris, it was to marry the daughter of the woman who, for all he knew, might well have been responsible for his mother's murder.

Henry, for all the fifty-six mistresses for whom he was later to become famous, was not a particularly prepossessing young man. His grandfather, Henry d'Albret, had brought him up until the age of 5 virtually as a peasant boy, running wild among the mountains, and he always retained rustic habits. Cleanliness was not his strong point: he was said to have a distinct aversion to water; the last letter his mother wrote him before her death exhorted him to make sure that there were no lice in his hair when he came for his wedding; and both Marguerite and his second wife, Marie de' Medici, complained that his breath always smelt of garlic. Marguerite, on the other hand, was a beautiful and very sophisticated young woman, lavishly dressed and with her naturally dark hair concealed under a wig of modish little blonde curls, who seems already to have had experience of a more elaborate and gallant kind of courtship than Henry of Navarre was likely to offer. Her name had been linked with that of the young and handsome Henry of Guise; indeed, the Spanish ambassador had reported that the relationship between them had progressed so far that Charles IX, Marguerite's unstable brother, had first of all ordered the assassination of Guise, and then, when that misfired, had physically attacked his sister in the early hours of the morning, frightening her so much that she had not recovered consciousness for more than an hour. Whether or not that was true, there was certainly an alarming incident at the wedding of Marguerite and Henry when, as Marguerite was asked for her consent to the marriage, Henry of Guise stood up from his place in the congregation and looked her full in the face. Seeing him, Marguerite stood dumbstruck until her brother Charles IX, determined that nothing should interfere with the marriage, leant across and hit her on the neck, so that her head jerked forward in a gesture of agreement.

Disturbing and unconventional though this was, it was by no means the most awkward feature of the wedding. In the initial stages of negotiation, both Catherine de' Medici and Jeanne d'Albret had hoped for a sudden conversion by the other party; but since Marguerite, despite her frivolity, was a genuinely pious Catholic, and Henry of Navarre's power base rested on the fact of his Protestantism, each had clung firmly to their own religion. This therefore produced the difficult situation of a wedding ceremony which had to be accommodated to the needs of two different religions. In the end, it was decided that the actual marriage should take place in the porch of the cathedral, in accordance with Huguenot practice, and that Marguerite should then proceed alone into the body of the church to hear mass. This already awkward arrangement was complicated still further by the fact that Henry, who appeared to be slightly drunk, did not wait for his bride in an orderly fashion, but paraded up and down on the porch talking to his friends and followers in a manner which showed little respect for the rite taking place inside.

All this was as nothing, however, to the dreadful aftermath of the marriage. Unbeknown to Marguerite, her mother, Catherine de' Medici, and her younger brother, Henry, Duke of Anjou, were heavily involved in a plot to counteract the growing power of the Huguenot leader Admiral Coligny, who they felt exerted a dangerously growing influence over the young King Charles IX. Knowing that Charles would never countenance the murder of his mentor, and unwilling to disrupt the arrangements for the marriage of Marguerite, they had worked in deepest secrecy, and had hired an assassin to do the work for them. Unfortunately, the assassin they chose, a man by the name of Maurevert, proved to be singularly bad at his job. At his first attempt to shoot the Admiral, he missed him and killed someone else instead; at his second attempt, he did indeed succeed in hitting Coligny, but only in the arm. When news came to Charles IX that his friend had been wounded he was most indignant, and immediately uttered loud threats against Coligny's enemy, the Duke of Guise, whom he assumed to be responsible for the attack. What he did not know, however, was that on this occasion both his mother and his brother were in league with the Guises, and that it was they who had instigated the attack on Coligny.

In the political turmoil of Paris, though, no one could expect to keep a secret for long. Catherine de' Medici knew that it was only a matter of time before Charles learned of the involvement of herself and Henry; and she also knew that Charles was bitterly jealous of his brother, who was much more glamorous than he was and had already been successful at some important military engagements, and was also generally considered to be their mother's favourite. Knowing of Charles's violent temper and his propensity to sudden, uncontrollable rages, she may well have thought it perfectly possible that Charles, when he learned the truth, might actually commit violence against his brother. She therefore decided to forestall any possible disclosure by their enemies by sending an envoy of her own to Charles to make a clean breast of the matter.

The envoy, a Florentine who had come with Catherine to France at the time of her marriage and had stayed with her ever since, did his job well. Not only did he succeed in making Charles realize that he had been presented with a *fait accompli*; he also persuaded him that the Huguenots were bound to want revenge for the injury to Coligny, and that they would blame not only Catherine and Henry but Charles himself for the attack on him. Therefore, he argued, if Charles did not wish to bring about the deaths of his mother and brother and quite probably of himself too, he had better act at once to forestall the insurrection which the Huguenots were undoubtedly planning to avenge the attack on Coligny.

Finding himself thus cornered, Charles went into one of the frantic rages for which he had become notorious. Fears for his own life and throne outweighed his affection for Coligny and for the party of which Coligny was the leader. 'Kill the lot! Kill the lot!' he shouted at his terrified councillors, and later, when they had rushed to carry out his order, he himself seized a firearm and shot from the windows of the palace at Huguenots running for shelter.

Thus began the St. Bartholomew's Day Massacre, the mass slaughter of Huguenots which began in Paris but was later to spread through the kingdom. It took place only four days after the marriage of Henry of Navarre and Marguerite, the alliance which had been supposed to bring unity between Catholics and Protestants, but which instead became known as the 'Bloodstained Wedding'. For Marguerite herself, caught completely by surprise by the turn of events, it was a terrifying experience. From the first, however, she seems to have had no doubt where her loyalties lay: in the conflict between her family and her husband, she would stick by her husband. The first she knew of the massacre was when she was woken from sleep to find a bloodstained and wounded follower of her husband's panting at her bedroom door, begging for rescue; wearing only her nightgown, she stood between him and the royal archers who were pursuing him until their captain agreed to grant her his life. Later she pleaded with her brother to spare her husband, which he eventually agreed to do, and despite her initial opposition to the marriage, she also refused to consider a divorce; when her mother Catherine de' Medici told her that if she would only say that her husband was impotent then an annulment could be arranged, she replied rather disingenuously that she was not sufficiently experienced to be able to tell. The young King of Navarre was therefore allowed to keep both his life and his bride, although he was forced to convert to Catholicism and had to remain a virtual prisoner at the French court.

Henry seems to have appreciated what his wife had done for him, and although he seems neither to have loved her nor, despite her famous beauty, to have found her particularly attractive, he treated her with respect and indulgence. She had very probably saved his life, and in return he appears to have accorded her the freedom to live her life however she wished. Most especially, he did not adhere to any kind of double standard in their marriage. He himself had no intention of remaining faithful to his wife; and she, similarly, took lovers without any apparent objection from Henry.

The first of these was a courtier from Provence, Joseph de Boniface de la Molle. He was handsome, sophisticated, and had already enjoyed numerous liaisons among the court ladies. But although Marguerite's husband might look with equanimity on La Molle's liaison with his wife, her brother, King Charles IX, did not. He had previously been scandalized by rumours of an affair between her and Henry of Guise; but this was even worse, because Guise at least had been high-born, whereas La Molle was not. After the failure of an attempt by the King to have him assassinated, La Molle was finally ensnared on a charge of having stuck pins into a wax model of Charles IX, who was by then on his deathbed, to ensure the succession to the throne of the Duke of Alençon, Marguerite's youngest brother, who was friendly with Henry of Navarre and was thought to favour the Huguenot cause. Navarre was also arraigned on this occasion, but Marguerite composed a plea to be read out in his defence, and, apparently as a result of it, he was spared punishment. La Molle, however, was not so lucky. After having his fingernails ripped off and his limbs crushed in a vain attempt to induce him to confess and implicate Navarre and Alençon, he was beheaded in front of a crowd which included many of his past mistresses, all in tears. His final message was 'Commend me to the good graces of the Queen of Navarre, and to all the ladies.' His head, as was usual, was publicly displayed, but that same night it was secretly removed. It was said that it was Marguerite's chamberlain who had taken it, and that she had personally carried it in her coach to receive a proper burial.

Although Marguerite grieved for her lover, she soon found another to replace him. This was Louis de Clermont, who was always known as Bussy after his domain of Bussy d'Amboise, who like La Molle was already famous as a courtier, a duellist and a lover. By this time Charles IX had died, and the new King was now Marguerite's other brother Henry III, who had been on bad terms with her since they were both children. According to Marguerite herself, Henry had frequently tried to disgrace her in the eyes of her mother and her husband, and had in fact succeeded in causing a coldness between her and Navarre. Henry was also very hostile to their youngest brother, Francis Duke of Alençon, who was a close friend of Marguerite and her husband and also of Bussy. Marguerite therefore regarded it as no coincidence that, shortly after her liaison with Bussy began, an attempt was made on his life. This proved unsuccessful, but Catherine de' Medici decided that in view of what had occurred Bussy should be asked to leave court. Thus Marguerite found herself once again deprived of a lover by the intervention of her family, and when, shortly afterwards, one of the King's gentlemen, who was said to have been instrumental in the attack on Bussy, was found murdered, it was widely alleged that this was Marguerite's revenge; she had, it was said, persuaded his assassin to do the deed by sleeping with him. Whatever the truth or falsity of this story, it indicates something of what Marguerite's reputation had by then become.

Shortly after the banishment of Bussy, Marguerite's youngest brother the Duke of Alençon at last succeeded in escaping from the court, where he had been held as a virtual prisoner, and soon after that, Henry of Navarre, too, escaped. Marguerite was immediately blamed by her brother Henry III for having helped the two men to escape, and was confined to her room; according to Marguerite, her brother was in fact so incensed that he even attempted to have her favourite lady-in-waiting drowned, and the poor girl was saved only in the nick of time. Fortunately for Marguerite, she had other interests beside love affairs: like her great-aunt the first Queen Marguerite of Navarre, she not only read a great deal but also wrote—in her case, poetry—and she was also fond of studying the classics, the scriptures and philosophy. She also kept up a clandestine correspondence with her husband by means of which he could be kept informed of the latest developments at the Valois court. She was also not forgotten by her youngest brother Francis of Alençon, who had used the time since his release in joining the forces which were fighting for political compromise. In this he was so successful that Henry III was soon forced to come to terms with him, and one of those terms was the immediate release from confinement of Marguerite, of whom Francis had always been very fond. Another clause also stipulated the posthumous rehabilitation of her first lover La Molle, and a third attempted to ensure that Marguerite would at last get the dowry which had been promised on her marriage but which had still not been paid.

Marguerite was, however, still not allowed to join her husband in Navarre: Henry III declared that her presence added too much glamour to his court for him to let her go. In fact, he was planning to avenge his humiliation at the hands of Alençon by declaring war on the Huguenots, Henry of Navarre included. Marguerite, however, refused to remain at a court which was at war with her husband, and therefore took up an offer from her brother Alençon of acting as his ambassadress on a visit to the Netherlands. The Netherlands had formed part of the Burgundian inheritance of the Emperor Charles V, and were accordingly ruled by Spain, but Spanish rule was deeply unpopular in both the Calvinist north Netherlands and the moderately Catholic south Netherlands. They were accordingly in a state of revolt against the Spanish king Philip II and his illegitimate half-brother, Don John, who had been appointed as their Governor. They wanted to appoint a new Governor, but the Protestant William of Orange, who was favoured by the Calvinists, was unacceptable to the moderate Catholics in the south. They therefore turned to Alençon, who had already distinguished himself as a moderate Catholic in French politics. Unable to go himself to negotiate with them, since he was still under such suspicion from the King, Alençon asked Marguerite to go instead and attempt to secure for him the position of Governor—a position which he hoped later to convert into a throne, in fulfilment of Nostradamus's prediction, by which all Catherine de' Medici's children were haunted, that they would all wear crowns. Pretending to be going to a spa in order to cure a rash on her arm, she obtained permission from her mother and brother to leave the court, and set off for the Netherlands to fulfil her secret mission.

Her embassy was not without its trials: being always on the move, she found it difficult to keep up with the constantly changing political situation both in the Netherlands and back home in France, and she also felt that she was in some danger of falling into the hands of the Spaniards, who could then attempt to use her as a hostage. At one place she received a hostile reception from the townspeople, and was very amused to discover that while they remained totally unmoved by the fact that she was the sister of the King of France and the sister-in-law of the King of Spain, they became instantly respectful when they learned that she was an acquaintance of their own local potentate. Nevertheless, she acquitted herself well enough for the hoped-for invitation for her brother to be forthcoming, so she returned in some triumph to France.

There Alençon greeted her with delight. Indeed, he seemed so pleased to see her again that gossips at the court of France hinted that the relationship between Marguerite and this youngest of her brothers was in fact incestuous; but the poor Alençon had in fact been left hideously deformed by a bout of smallpox, which had given him the unfortunate appearance of having two noses, and seemed unlikely to be able to attract anyone at all, let alone a beauty like his sister. Certainly Marguerite showed no inclination to stay with Alençon, but immediately resumed her campaign to be allowed to join her husband in Navarre. Navarre might be only a poor provincial kingdom; but at least her husband had shown her respect and had allowed her, very largely, to have her own way, whereas she trusted neither her mother nor her brother King Henry III and found her movements very much hampered by them. But escaping from them was not to prove so easy. Despite Marguerite's pleas to go to Navarre and those of her brother Alençon to take up the Governorship which had been offered to him in the Netherlands, neither of them could obtain permission to leave the court, and both had to stay in Paris.

There they and their circle lived in a state of tacit warfare with Henry III and his *mignons*. On one occasion when the King and his favourites had appeared in particularly lavish costume, their hair curled and scented and their elaborate lace collars open to show their chests, Marguerite's lover Bussy, now back at court and in the service of Alençon, entered dressed as plainly as possible, but accompanied by pages clad in gold, saying loudly that the less important people were at court, the more ostentatiously they dressed. Bussy sailed even closer to the wind when, ordered to reconcile himself with a favourite of Henry III's by a ceremonial embrace, he jeeringly went one step further and bestowed on him a lingering kiss.

Soon the hostility between the two factions came to a head and Alençon found himself placed under guard. He begged for Marguerite to share his incarceration; she loved him so much, he said, that he knew she would be glad to. Marguerite justified his faith by agreeing to share his imprisonment, and later, when the intervention of their mother Catherine de' Medici had secured their partial release, Marguerite put herself still further at risk by aiding her brother to escape from the palace by a rope let down from her bedroom window.

She escaped punishment for this, however, because her mother and brother now had a use for her. It was becoming increasingly obvious that Henry III would have no children, and Alençon, the heir to the throne, was sickly. It was looking very likely, therefore, that Marguerite's husband Henry of Navarre would one day succeed to the throne of France, and Catherine de' Medici, anxious to avoid the Catholic rebellion that would undoubtedly break out at the prospect of a Huguenot King, had decided to make a further attempt to convert Navarre to Catholicism. For Marguerite, this was good news; the only rôle she had been able to carve out for herself at court was as the helper of her youngest brother Alençon, and now that he was no longer there she was left isolated and without any obvious position to fill, whereas at the court of Navarre she would be Queen, and could also hope that one day, when her brother Henry III died, she would be Queen of France too. But there were still problems ahead. It was two and a half years since she had seen her husband; in that time, he was known to have had many mistresses, and after the treatment meted out to his co-religionists by Henry III the welcome which he would offer to the King's sister might perhaps be doubtful. Courtiers who accompanied the magnificent procession of Marguerite and her mother Catherine de' Medici as it travelled slowly down to Navarre reported back that Marguerite was spending many hours on perfecting her physical appearance, having her eyebrows carefully plucked, scenting herself with frequent baths, and devoting much attention to her hair and clothes.

All her preparations, however, could not alter the fact that the Wars of Religion had placed a serious breach between her and her husband. It was hard even to find a town in which the Protestant retinue of the King and the Catholic retinue of the Queen could both be accommodated without causing trouble, and there was also difficulty when Marguerite, who had been given permission to hear private Masses, allowed some of the local Catholics into her chapel, only to find them immediately arrested by servants of her husband. Nevertheless, she and Navarre were soon able to resume the easy-going system of living almost separate private lives which they had established at the French court. Marguerite devoted much time and energy to furnishing and adornment of her new court, at Nérac, capital of Navarre, while Henry entertained himself with a succession of mistresses. Marguerite, too, took lovers, much to the horror of the Protestant ministers of her husband's little country. Her first affair in her new home was with a friend of her husband's, the Viscount of Turenne, but it ended when he left to lead the Huguenot army in renewed fighting against the Catholics. He was soon replaced, however, by the great love of Marguerite's life:

Jacques de Harlay, Marquis de Chanvallon.

Chanvallon was a year or so younger than Marguerite, who was now nearing 30, and he was said to be the most handsome man of his day. He also shared Marguerite's own taste for poetry, and himself composed verses. If Marguerite had been indiscreet in her love affairs before, this time she threw caution to the winds; her infatuation soon became common knowledge, and immediately reached the ears of her brother, King Henry III. He was already displeased with her—he blamed her for not having been able to influence her husband sufficiently to prevent the renewal of fighting between Catholics and Huguenots, and also thought that she had been dilatory in attempting to negotiate a peace between the two sides—and now his behaviour towards her became even colder. To add to Marguerite's troubles, Chanvallon, who was Master of Horse to her younger brother the Duke of Alençon, found himself having to accompany the Duke to Flanders. Still making no secret of her passion, Marguerite attired herself in black, as though she had been widowed, and spent her time reading the classics and writing love-letters to the absent Chanvallon.

By now her behaviour was becoming notorious. Rumours spread that she was carrying Chanvallon's child; they were untrue, but as well as publicizing the news of her adultery, they also drew attention to another problem in her life: the fact that she had never been pregnant at all. Even a child of doubtful fatherhood could well have strengthened her position, since she herself was of the royal blood of France and therefore any child she produced could be guaranteed to be royal on one side at least; but the absence of any heir at all constituted a considerable threat to the succession. Her failure to conceive was underlined when her husband's mistress, a young woman known as Fosseuse, became pregnant, and also succeeded in bringing about a breach between Marguerite and her husband Henry. Fortunately for Marguerite, Fosseuse's child, a girl, was born dead, but the episode of the pregnancy, the estrangement between her and her husband, and the absence of her lover, made Marguerite decide temporarily to leave her husband's court. She took Fosseuse with her to Paris, and once there lost no time in dismissing the unfortunate girl from the royal service. Thus she had rid herself of a potentially dangerous enemy, and now that she was away from her husband she could not only hope that absence would soften his recent animosity towards her, but she could also once again attempt to establish herself as his valuable informant at her brother's court.

The situation in Paris had changed, though, since Marguerite had been there last. During her absence her brother Henry III had acquired two more *mignons*, the Duke of Joyeuse and the Duke of Epernon. They were immensely powerful and influential, and, aware of Henry's resentment towards his sister and his displeasure at her well-publicized affairs, they lost no time in letting her know that they were her enemies. She retaliated by attempting to win over as many as possible of the King's *mignons* to having affairs with her ladies, in an attempt to spite her brother. As well as this near-public war between her and the King, she also suffered a personal blow when her lover Chanvallon decided that his financial affairs required him to contract a marriage with a wealthy widow. She forgave him, though, when he returned to Paris saying that the marriage had made him unhappy; she told him that she could understand this only too easily, for her own marriage had been the cause of all the suffering in her life. She continued, though, to suffer jealousy over his relations with other women, perhaps exacerbated by the bitter knowledge that she herself was losing her looks, and that her once-lovely figure was thickening and coarsening. She was no longer what she had once been, an ornament to her brother's court; in fact she was now nothing more than an irritant to him. After one particularly bad quarrel, when she had refused to comply with his request that she should dismiss two of her ladies-in-waiting, he ordered her to leave the capital.

This was a grave insult, but it was merely the start of Marguerite's downfall. Although her brother had been thwarted in his attempt to arrest Chanvallon by the timely escape of the latter, he was nevertheless able to detain a number of his sister's retainers and have them interrogated about her immoral life and whether or not she had borne any illegitimate children. Marguerite was openly, irrevocably disgraced. She knew that Chanvallon, who had escaped to Germany, would never be permitted to see her again; and she herself was left with nowhere to go, for not only had her brother cast her off and publicly humiliated her, but her husband, who had by now found himself a new mistress to replace the banished Fosseuse, had decided to hold his brother-in-law to ransom by refusing to receive Marguerite back at his court unless her brother could clear her name of the accusations he had made against her. Now that she had been disgraced in this way, Navarre declared, it would be a smirch on his own honour to acknowledge her as his wife again until her good name was restored, and he was encouraged in this attitude by his new mistress Corisande, who hoped that if the Queen was repudiated by her husband then maybe she herself could take her place. Navarre's own motives were rather different: he was proposing not to take Marguerite back until her brother had offered him military concessions. So, while the bargaining between the two Kings went on, Marguerite, caught between the two sides, progressed slowly and miserably southwards, until negotiations were finally completed and she was allowed to return to her husband, where she spent her first evening back at court sitting neglected by his side, not spoken to by anybody and weeping copiously throughout the evening.

She had hardly had time to recover herself from the effects of her humiliating journey when a fresh disaster overtook her. The one member of her family to whom she had remained close was her younger brother Francis, Duke of Alençon. Although he had been away in Flanders for some time, she had always known that she had his support. But for some time Francis had been visibly sickening from tuberculosis. Now, still only 30 years old, he died.

Marguerite suffered both personally and politically from the death of her favourite brother. He had been the one person left to her whom she felt she could still trust; but even more than that, now that he was dead the new heir to the throne of France was her own husband, Henry of Navarre. This meant that her brother Henry III and her mother Catherine de' Medici were forced to seek friendship with Navarre if the kingdom was not to be pulled apart. Much of the little power which remained to Marguerite depended on her value as a possible go-between between her husband and her brother; but now that circumstances had driven them to it, they set about forging an understanding from which she was excluded. At the same time she also began to feel, whether rightly or not, that she was personally under threat from the machinations of her husband's mistress, Corisande, who she felt might poison her in order to be able to take her place. Feeling that her last hope of retrieving her position was to produce a son, she undertook a pilgrimage to pray that she might become pregnant. Of that, however, there was little chance. Moved partly by the persuasions of Corisande and partly by Marguerite's own infidelity, Henry of Navarre made it clear to her that she could never give him a child now, for he did not propose to sleep with her again in case she should then use that as an excuse to foist a bastard onto him.

Marguerite's situation now appeared hopeless. She felt, however, that there was still one possibility open to her. Alarmed by the growing rapprochement between Henry III and Henry of Navarre, and by the growing likelihood that the next King of France would be a Huguenot, Marguerite's old admirer Henry of Guise had decided to launch a Catholic League which, with the help of Philip of Spain, would fight to exclude Henry of Navarre from the throne and, very probably, put Henry of Guise himself there instead. Marguerite had never liked her brother Henry III, and was now completely estranged from her husband Henry of Navarre; Henry of Guise, on the other hand, was an old flame of hers. She therefore decided to intervene in his favour in what was becoming known as the War of the Three Henries.

Telling her husband that she was going to pass Easter in the Catholic city of Agen, which was part of the territories which had been gifted to her on her marriage, she left court. She did indeed go to Agen—but once there she filled it with soldiers, and declared that she was holding it for the Catholic League. In the same gesture she had made herself a traitor to both her husband and her brother, and if her desperate gamble was unsuccessful, she could expect retribution from either side if she were unlucky enough to be captured.

She failed to realize, however, that she was not the only

person caught in a terrible predicament: the people of Agen were suffering too. They had to endure the Queen tearing down their houses in order to build military emplacements, and there were also several incidents of rape and pillaging by Marguerite's ill-disciplined soldiers. The final straw came when plague broke out in the city. Despite the daily deaths, Marguerite refused to acknowledge its existence, claiming that it was a rumour spread by the Huguenots to wear down her resistance, and she forbade the townspeople to attempt to escape from it by fleeing into the countryside. Provoked beyond endurance, they appealed to Henry III to save them from his sister, blew up the convent where she was staying and would very probably have killed her, if she had not been rescued in the nick of time.

Although Marguerite had so little endeared herself to the townspeople, she still, even at a rather dumpy 32, possessed enough of her old magic to have been able to fascinate two of her commanding officers, two unsophisticated, soldierly men named Aubiac and Lignerac. Aubiac had almost certainly become her lover; Lignerac had not, but was nevertheless sufficiently devoted to her to engineer her escape from the furious mob and cover her retreat while, riding pillion behind a soldier in considerable physical discomfort, she escaped to the tiny fortress of Carlat, another of the properties she had received in her marriage treaty, which was commanded by Lignerac's brother, de Marzé.

Marguerite appeared to have been miraculously saved. Soon, however, she realized that her deliverance was less of a blessing than it had at first seemed. When Lignerac arrived from Agen to join his brother at Carlat, it gradually became obvious to Marguerite that the two were acting less in her interest than in her brother's, and that she was, in fact, a virtual prisoner at Carlat. The strain told on her health and soon made her very ill indeed, so that for weeks she was in a state of high fever and her life was despaired of. In such a remote place the only person available to nurse her was the son of the local apothecary, who performed the task so well that Marguerite not only did not die, but gradually regained her health and strength.

Not everyone in the castle was enjoying good health,

however. De Marzé, one of her two jailers, suddenly sickened and died, giving rise to the rumour that Marguerite, who was thought to have been taught about poisons by her Italian mother Catherine de' Medici, had murdered him. This was bad enough, but it was followed almost immediately by an even more scandalous incident: Lignerac, the surviving brother, decided that Marguerite, to whom he himself was attracted, had taken the young boy who had nursed her as her lover, and in a fit of jealous rage he stabbed the lad to death in the presence of Marguerite herself, 'so close to her bed that she was covered with bloodstains'. Like her sister-in-law Mary, Queen of Scots, another Queen who gave rise to much scandal in her own day, was widely believed to be guilty of adultery, and had her so-called lover David Rizzio murdered in her presence, Marguerite had been soiled now not only by scandal but also by blood.

Even now, however, Marguerite still had left to her the young soldier Aubiac, who had commanded part of her forces at Agen and whom she had taken for her lover there. The first time Aubiac had ever seen her he had exclaimed, 'Let me be hanged, if I might only once sleep with that woman', and his devotion had been unswerving ever since. Lignerac was jealous of him, too, and had even threatened to have Aubiac thrown from the battlements; but Marguerite appeased him—probably by agreeing at last to sleep with him—and was thus eventually able to escape, with Aubiac's help, from the gloomy fortress that had been her prison. She had decided to go to the castle of Ibois, which had once been offered to her by her mother. The journey was both hazardous and exhausting; but worse was to come, for when Marguerite finally arrived at Ibois she discovered why it had been so easy for her to escape from Carlat. She had walked into a trap, set for her by her brother King Henry III.

She herself was safe from the ultimate punishment of death. The wife of a King might well be executed for treason in the sixteenth century, as indeed happened to two of the Queens of Henry VIII; but Marguerite was also the daughter and sister of Kings, and as such she was safe. The unfortunate Aubiac, however, had no such guarantee. Marguerite's liaison with him had scandalized the Valois court because he was not even of noble blood, and her brother and mother had also been appalled by the rumour, untrue but widely current, that she had borne him a deaf-and-dumb child. Marguerite attempted to smuggle him out of Ibois in women's clothing; but she failed. Aubiac was captured and, to mark the poor opinion held of him by the King and the Queen Mother, he was denied the gentleman's death of beheading and was, instead, hanged, upside down. He was then cut down before he was quite dead and was thrown into his grave, still living and still holding, it was said, a muff of Marguerite's.

Little was now left for Marguerite. Her mother and brother, feeling that she had heaped disgrace upon their heads, even went so far as to suggest to her husband Henry of Navarre that if he would oblige them by converting to Catholicism, they in turn could oblige him by having Marguerite put into a convent. There was even a hint that they might, if necessary, be willing to hasten her death, albeit not publicly; and Catherine de' Medici, ever a believer in matrimonial diplomacy, had a new wife for Henry already marked out, in the shape of her grand-daughter Christine of Lorraine. When Henry refused this marriage, however, Catherine realized that it would in fact be better to keep Marguerite alive, and also still married to Henry, since if he were free to marry again his next wife might well be a Protestant one. Marguerite was therefore sent to the forbidding castle of Usson to be kept as a prisoner there.

But even in this blackest hour Marguerite still had her charm and her resourcefulness, which she immediately set to work on her jailer and his wife. In this she was phenomenally successful; almost incredibly, her jailer surrendered the castle to her and, as a result of her persuasion, himself went off to fight for the Catholic League led by her early admirer the Duke of Guise. Marguerite had triumphed. The only disadvantage of her position was that she had to remain in the gloomy backwater of Usson, but that did at least have compensations in that it kept her out of the hurly-burly of politics, which just at that time was proving to be a remarkably dangerous occupation in terms of its cost in lives. The first death within Marguerite's own family was the execution of Mary, Queen of Scots, who had once been her sister-in-law and whose story had so many similarities to her own; then France was shaken when her brother Henry III had his two most dangerous rivals, Marguerite's old flame the Duke of Guise and his brother the Cardinal of Lorraine, assassinated. This rash act also proved the death-knell of the old Queen Mother, Catherine de' Medici, who expired soon after; and the catalogue of disasters was finally completed when, in a revenge attack for the murder of Guise, Henry III himself was stabbed to death by a monk. His death left Henry of Navarre as King of France in his place; and Marguerite herself was now Queen.

Queen only in name, however, for her husband did not send for her to join him, and indeed he himself was having considerable trouble exerting his authority over a kingdom which was not prepared to accept a Huguenot ruler. The only real difference in Marguerite's situation was that now that both her mother and brother were dead, she could live a rather freer life than she had been doing of late. Supported by an income which was rather improbably provided for her by her saintly sister-in-law Elisabeth of Austria, wife of her late brother Charles IX, she surrounded herself with as much luxury as she could manage and proceeded to take a series of lovers. They were not quite in the same league, in terms of looks, pedigree and accomplishments, as the splendid cavaliers of her youth, but then Marguerite herself was no longer the beauty she had once been: her weight problem, caused perhaps by some kind of glandular or thyroid problem, was becoming ever more severe. She busied herself with reading and also with writing her memoirs, which the Académie Française were later to consider amongst the masterpieces of French literature. It was really all that there was left for her to do, for although Queen in name, she was very far from being Queen in fact.

Henry of Navarre, now Henry IV of France, had long since ceased to regard her as his Queen. He was in fact anxious to marry his mistress, the beautiful Gabrielle d'Estrées, in the hope that he could legitimize his two children by her, his only sons Caesar and Alexander, and declare them the heirs to the crown. Marguerite had little objection to the plan; she knew that she could never hope to be reconciled with her husband and be received as Queen, and she was, in any case, happy enough at Usson with her lovers. She showed no animosity towards Gabrielle d'Estrées, and indeed went so far as to say that she would make the two boys, Caesar and Alexander, her heirs. She would put no obstacles in the way of the divorce, which, because Henry had no desire to raise a scandal by accusing his wife of adultery, was to be sued for on the grounds that she had been forced into the marriage by her family and had never been truly consenting to it. The one thing Marguerite did insist on was money; and that was, too, the one thing that Henry did not have. Negotiations over her allowance dragged on so long that it was not until ten years after the death of her brother Henry III that Marguerite finally received the funds she had been promised and petitioned the Pope to end her marriage. After that, however, there were no more delays. The Pope was only too glad to free her husband Henry to marry a more suitable wife who could confirm him in the Catholicism that he had been recently, and reluctantly, forced to adopt to ensure his recognition as King throughout the kingdom. Marguerite was to be allowed to keep her title as Queen of Navarre, but she was no longer Queen of France.

Henry's original intention had been to crown his mistress Gabrielle d'Estrées in her stead, but before the divorce came through, Gabrielle had died of a stroke after giving birth to a still-born child. Henry had therefore to look around for a new Queen, and his choice fell on Marie de' Medici, a distant relative of Marguerite's mother Catherine de' Medici who was, as Catherine herself had been, a niece of the Pope, and could therefore bring Henry valuable Catholic support. And where Marguerite de Valois had failed, Marie de' Medici succeeded triumphantly: nine months after the marriage, a son, Louis, was born. France had an heir at last.

One of the earliest letters of congratulation came from Marguerite herself. Now that she and Henry were divorced, there were no longer any grounds for contention between them, and they were on as good terms as they had been when they were first married. They addressed each other as brother and sister; she declared the new Dauphin her legal heir. Henry even allowed her to leave Usson, which had been her home for twenty years now, and take up residence near the court, so that she could once again be surrounded by the gaiety and luxury she loved. Also for the first time in twenty years, she met her former husband again, and at once settled down into a very comfortable relationship with him, with his wife, who became a great friend to her, and above all with the little Dauphin, her heir, whom she treated like a son, and who returned her affection. The closeness of her new relationship with the King was underlined when her current lover, a young man many years her junior, was shot dead in front of her by a youth who bore him a grudge. Marguerite should not fret, said the King; she might have lost one lover, but there were plenty of other good-looking young men at court, and he would be very happy to put a dozen or so of them at her service.

She did not, however, need to take advantage of his offer; plump and elderly though she had become, her glamour was still sufficient to attract the attentions of a young man named Bajaumont, who immediately became her new lover. By now, however, this was a rather taxing rôle: Marguerite demanded endless attention and was fiercely jealous, and King Henry was soon writing to his wife Marie de' Medici, '. . . yesterday Queen Marguerite beat Bajaumont, and he wants to leave.' When Bajaumont died young of tuberculosis, Paris gossip blamed it on Marguerite's sexual rapaciousness. But even this last bereavement did not deter Marguerite: she took another lover, a young man named Villars, and took to making him wear clothes of the style that had been fashionable among the young men of her girlhood, which led to him being unmercifully teased by the rest of the court. Since she herself had now become popularly known as 'Queen Margot', Villars was derisively termed 'King Margot'. He did, however, seem to be genuinely attached to her; when she was ill he vowed that if she recovered he would perform a pilgrimage on foot, and when she was better he duly set out to perform it—with Marguerite, unable to manage without him, going too, in a coach driven at walking-pace.

Soon, however, she was back at court, to fulfil an important ceremonial function. Marie de' Medici, although she had by now presented the King with a numerous family of children, had never really felt that her position was secure, since Henry was so much given to passionate love affairs and might, having already divorced one wife, perhaps get the same idea again. She therefore pleaded for a coronation, which would definitely install her as Queen of France, and finally Henry yielded and arranged one for her. At this coronation Marguerite too would be present, the last of the Valois symbolically walking with the first of the Bourbons. In fact it was the last time that Marguerite was ever to see her former husband. The next day he was assassinated, leaving Marie de' Medici a widow and the young Dauphin Louis King of France.

Now that they had both been bereaved, Marguerite and Marie de' Medici drew closer than ever. But Marguerite was ageing now. Five years after the death of her former husband, in 1615, she too died. Marie de' Medici was left to struggle on alone as Regent, making numerous political mistakes along the way; the last of the great Queens of France, daughter, sister and wife of Kings, was dead.

IV

Mothers of Sons

NONE of the Queens Consort of Spain had a life as varied or as exciting as that of Marguerite of Valois. The wife whom the much-betrothed Emperor Charles V, King of Spain, eventually chose was his beautiful cousin Isabella of Portugal, daughter of his mother's sister, a serious, dignified and deeply pious woman. One of the qualities which had initially recommended her to Charles was that, being half-Spanish, she would make a good Regent of Spain during the periods when he was away in the other parts of his vast territories, and this was a rôle that she fulfilled admirably. Isabella, like her husband, took her duties and her royal position very seriously: during the thirteen hours of painful labour that she endured at the birth of her first child, she asked her attendants to put a veil over her face so that no one would see her suffering, and told them, 'I may die, but I will not cry out.' She was devoted to her husband and family, interesting herself personally in the education of her children in a way that was unusual for sixteenth-century Queens, and they returned her affection. They were devastated when, with her eldest son still only 12, Isabella fell ill and died. The bereaved Emperor Charles retreated to a monastery for two months and grieved, while her son Philip had to escort his mother's body on the long journey in the hot summer to Spain to its final resting place in Granada. Not surprisingly, the body did not travel well: indeed, the official who received it at the other end was so shocked by the state of it when he opened the coffin that he promptly entered a monastery.

Four years later, when Isabella's son Philip reached the age of 16, he, too, took a wife from Portugal: Maria Manuela, daughter of Isabella's brother Juan. The marriage was arranged by Philip's father the Emperor Charles, who was, however, anxious that his son should not see too much of his wife: sexual intercourse, he grimly warned his son, was highly dangerous and could even lead to death, and should be indulged in only in order to produce heirs and never for enjoyment. This piece of advice might well have been prompted by the fact that the death of Charles's uncle, the young prince Juan, had been ascribed by his doctors to the fact that he had had too frequent relations with his wife Margaret of Austria; and Philip certainly seems to have taken it to heart, for not only was he almost unique amongst sixteenth-century Kings in having no mistresses at all, but all his subsequent wives were said to have been perturbed at his apparent lack of desire to sleep with them except when he felt that it was his duty.

Despite Charles's advice, however, the marriage did produce a child—a son, Don Carlos, called after Philip's father. But the young Maria Manuela did not survive the birth, and Philip, still only 18, was left a widower.

He did not marry again for nine years, and when he did it was to another cousin, Mary Tudor, daughter of his father's aunt Katherine of Aragon, who had recently become Queen Mary I of England. The marriage had numerous potential advantages, for not only was England the major trading partner of the Emperor Charles's domains in the Low Countries, but also any son of Philip and Mary would be able to add the crown of England to the vast collection of territories already ruled by Charles. On Mary's part, the motivation was primarily to find a powerful Catholic husband who could assist her politically in her attempts to reintroduce Catholicism into England, and who could also console her personally for all the many indignities she had suffered since the divorce of her mother Katherine of Aragon.

The marriage, however, was not a success. Mary was nine years older than Philip, and had been aged and embittered by the hardships she had had to endure. A portrait of her had been sent to her prospective bridegroom; but when Philip saw her in the flesh, he confided to his entourage that he would never trust painting again. Although he was created King of England in the right of his wife, he resolved to spend as little time there as possible, especially as he did not think that Mary would conceive. She did in fact believe herself pregnant; but it proved to be dropsy instead. Philip departed for the Netherlands, which became his property following first the abdication and then the death of his father, and Mary was left alone, childless, abandoned, and suffering from a fatal illness. Still hoping for Philip's return, she died with her prayer-book open at the ceremony for women recently recovered from childbirth.

Philip's third wife, who, now that his father was dead, was in fact the first to be Queen of Spain, was Elisabeth of Valois, daughter of Henry II of France and of Catherine de' Medici, and elder sister of Marguerite of Navarre. By the time of this third marriage, Philip was urgently in need of a son. He did, it was true, already have one, Don Carlos, from his first marriage to Maria Manuela; but the mental health of Don Carlos had been deteriorating for some time, and now it did not appear that he would ever be fit to rule. Part of the problem may well have lain in the growing Habsburg habit of intermarrying with their cousins, especially given the family history of serious mental imbalance: Philip's grandmother was, after all, Juana the Mad, and both Philip himself and Don Carlos's mother Maria Manuela were also descended from Juana's grandmother, the mad Queen Isabella of Portugal. At first the only signs that all was not well with the prince were his extreme slowness in learning to read and write, and his proneness to attacks of fever. Then when he was 17 years old he had a bad fall down a flight of stairs, leaving him blinded for a time and paralysed for six months. He was trepanned, which appears to have saved his life, but from then on he would fly frequently into wild rages in which he was quite inaccessible to reason. Philip, a deeply conscientious ruler who cared greatly about the fate of his many territories, agonized about what sort of a King Carlos would make and appeared to be searching for some way of denying him the succession. Then the King's hand was forced when his bastard half-brother, Don John of Austria, informed him that Don Carlos was secretly plotting to escape from the court and might, indeed, be planning the murder of his father.

Philip had his son arrested and ordered that he should be locked up in the same tower where the mad Queen Isabella of Portugal had once been confined, with the son of Juana the Mad's keeper as his jailer. Imprisonment did nothing to improve the prince's temper or behaviour, and he aggravated his condition further by going on hunger strike. Soon after his arrest, he was dead.

By the time of Don Carlos's death, Philip had already been married for eight years to his third wife Elisabeth de Valois. Almost twenty years younger than her husband, she had been still a child at the time of the marriage, so for the first two years it could not be consummated. Even when the King did begin to sleep with his wife, it was reported at court that he did not do so as often as she wished; that Philip, who seems to have regarded sex merely as a duty, would often not come at all to the room where she lay awake waiting for him, or, if he did come, would wait until late into the night, when he knew that she would probably have fallen asleep, so that he could tell himself that he had at least made the attempt. When after four years of marriage there had been only one rumour of a pregnancy, which turned out to be false, Philip, partly spurred on by the worsening of Don Carlos's condition, decided to make a serious effort. Instead of the one or two hours a day which was all that he could normally spare from government business, he decided to devote his time completely to his wife. A pregnancy, genuine this time, soon resulted; but only a month or so later the Queen fell ill, and the medical treatment of the day, consisting mainly of blood-letting and enemas, rapidly brought on a miscarriage and left the young Queen herself hovering on the point of death. An Italian doctor saved her, but her recovery was slow, and it was nearly two years before she became pregnant again.

This time the baby was born alive and healthy; but it was a girl, christened Isabella Clara Eugenia. Another pregnancy soon followed, but it too produced only a daughter, Catalina Micaela. Elisabeth, however, was still only 21 years old, and had now fully recovered from the effects of her earlier miscarriage. Soon she was pregnant again.

As in her first pregnancy, however, things did not go well. The Queen became very low-spirited, and was given to frequent fits of trembling and fainting. Once again, the doctors decided to intervene, with the same treatment which had so nearly been fatal on the previous occasion. Once again, Elisabeth miscarried—of yet another daughter—and died later that day.

The King was heartbroken. Elisabeth's death followed very closely on that of Don Carlos—so closely, indeed, that later gossip said that the Queen and the prince, who were very fond of each other, had been in love, and that Philip, discovering this, had had them both murdered out of jealousy. The King's grief at Elisabeth's death, however, did not bear out such a theory. Indeed, he was so distressed by losing her that he refused, at first, to consider remarriage, rebuffing utterly the suggestion of Elisabeth's mother Catherine de' Medici that he should marry her younger daughter, Elisabeth's sister, the beautiful and lively Marguerite de Valois. Eventually, however, his pressing need for a male heir to succeed him made him choose a fourth wife.

This time, as he had done in his first and second marriages, he conformed to the custom which was rapidly becoming established in the House of Habsburg of marrying within the family. His new wife was Anna of Austria, whose mother, Maria, was the King's own sister, and whose father, the Emperor Maximilian II, was the King's first cousin, making Anna both cousin and niece to her own husband. At the same time, he took under his wing some of Anna's brothers, encouraging them to spend time with him in Spain, obviously in the hope that, if he still failed to produce a son, one of his Austrian nephews would be fitted to succeed him. Meanwhile, court gossip reported that, unusually for him, Philip was sleeping every night in the Queen's bedroom, though whether he was actually making love to her or not it was impossible to say, since the Queen, like her husband but unusually in sixteenth-century royalty, was reticent about such matters. He must, however, had been doing so fairly frequently, for, unlike his other marriages, this one was markedly fruitful. As well as taking care of the King's two small daughters by Elisabeth of Valois, Anna of Austria also produced seven children of her own. Two of them were stillborn, but one daughter and three sons survived into infancy. Only one of those sons, however—the future Philip III—survived the rigours of childhood. The rest died in boyhood, but fortunately their mother was spared the grief of two of the three deaths, for she herself died ten years after her marriage of influenza.

The wives of Philip II suffered a high casualty rate, but all died from natural causes. The same, however, could not be said of the Queens of England. That was the country in which the pitfalls and perils of being a sixteenth-century Queen Consort were most clearly illustrated.

When Henry VIII first came to the throne in 1509, he was a young and splendid prince, handsome, well-educated, and hugely popular by comparison with his parsimonious father, whose court in his later years had often been a drab and joyless place. Henry saw himself as a romantic, knightly figure from the splendid world of chivalry, and the first act of his reign certainly gave assistance to a lady in distress. This was the princess Katherine of Aragon, who had been briefly married to Henry's elder brother, Prince Arthur. Arthur had died only months after the wedding; but Katherine had been a great catch for Henry's father King Henry VII, and he had been unwilling to let go of her easily. For one thing, the Tudor family's claim to the throne was questionable, since it depended on illegitimate descent from John of Gaunt; but not only was Katherine's own ancestry studded with royalty, but she could also claim *legitimate* descent from John of Gaunt through his second marriage, which would in turn strengthen the Tudor claim. Moreover, Katherine's father, Ferdinand of Aragon, was a wily, devious man, by whom Henry VII had often found himself outsmarted, but whose alliance he desperately needed. To hold Ferdinand's daughter as a virtual hostage offered a useful way of ensuring his co-operation.

Henry VII did not, however, want to commit himself. He hoped to keep Ferdinand dangling and to leave his own options open; so although he proposed a marriage between the widowed Katherine and his younger son Henry, which gave him a good reason to keep the girl in England, he did not actually proceed with it, and even instructed his son to lodge a formal objection to the betrothal in case he might at any time wish to be released from it. Meanwhile, Katherine was kept in England, short of money and facing a deeply uncertain future. It was a considerable test of her character that she was able to cope with her position, and even to put it to some use by acting as her father's *de facto* ambassadress in England. Although on one or two occasions she jeopardized her position by making political mistakes, she emerged, on the whole, with honour from the six long years of her widowhood.

Then they were suddenly ended. Her father-in-law, Henry VII, who had treated her so shabbily, died; Henry VIII succeeded him, and at once announced his intention of honouring the engagement he had earlier entered into and marrying his brother's widow, Katherine of Aragon. After the gravity of Henry VII's later years, the court suddenly burst into life, with elaborate entertainments and much feasting and dancing. In all this, Katherine participated willingly, demonstrating obliging surprise whenever her husband played his favourite game of putting on some outlandish disguise and bursting into her room with a crowd of followers, defying her to guess who he was. Although she was six years older than he, she was still only 24, and although never a great beauty, she had a pleasant appearance and a dignified carriage. In those early years the marriage was very much of a success. Katherine no doubt knew that her husband had mistresses; but that was nothing to her, for she was the Queen.

Her position became even stronger when, early in the marriage, she produced a son. There were tremendous rejoicings, because the Tudors were a new dynasty, still insecure on the throne, who desperately needed strong, healthy male heirs of undoubted legitimacy. The arrival of the baby prince Henry sent his father into an ecstasy of happiness. But the child was not strong; and only months later, he was dead. Other pregnancies followed, but ended in stillbirth. Only one of the children of Henry and Katherine lived; and that was not a son but a daughter, Mary, who, however fond her father might be of her, was useless to him as an heir. No woman had succeeded to the English throne since the Empress Matilda had tried, and failed, to do so in the twelfth century. Matilda's attempt to claim the crown had led to nineteen years of civil war—and, unless he had a son, that was exactly the fate that Henry feared for England after his death.

Katherine, however, seems to have been less dissatisfied

105

to have produced only a daughter. Herself the daughter of a Queen regnant, Isabella of Castile, she was unlikely to see any reason why a woman should not be able to succeed to the crown; and so her principal concern was to see that Mary received an education and training suitable to the heiress of England. But even while Katherine was thus planning for her daughter's future, it was becoming increasingly obvious that Henry VIII's mind was running along very different lines.

His affair with his mistress, Elizabeth Blount, had produced a son, whom Henry had christened Henry Fitzroy (Fitzroy, the Norman French for 'son of the King', being the standard surname for the bastards of Kings). The boy seemed a promising youth and Henry was fond of him; so, as it became clear that Katherine of Aragon was reaching the end of her childbearing years and Henry could no longer hope for a son from her, he began to move towards the possibility of declaring Fitzroy his heir. He created the boy Duke of Richmond, which was, significantly enough, the title which Henry's father Henry VII had borne before his accession to the throne, and at one stage he even contemplated marrying the boy to his half-sister Mary, Henry's legitimate daughter by Katherine of Aragon. This would have been incest, but the two together might be better able to enforce a claim to the throne than either jointly. But the Tudor claim to the throne had always been shaky, and to attempt to put forward an illegitimate child as the lawful heir might just succeed in destabilizing it altogether. There was, however, an alternative: to seek a divorce from Katherine, and to take a second wife, in the hope that she would be able to bear him legitimate sons.

Henry was encouraged in his ideas of divorce by his chief minister, Cardinal Wolsey, who had always favoured the French over the Spanish and now hoped that his master would be able to rid himself of his Aragonese wife and marry a French princess instead. Wolsey therefore set himself to the task of persuading the Pope to free the King by granting the divorce.

There were, however, two serious complications to the business. For a King to ask for a divorce from his wife on the grounds that she could not give him sons was by no means without precedent, and was usually achieved with little difficulty; the twelfth-century Louis VII of France had been allowed to divorce his wife Eleanor of Aquitaine for such a reason, and more recently Louis XII of France, who had married Henry's own sister Mary Tudor, had earlier divorced his first wife Jeanne of France for childlessness. Under normal circumstances, then, Henry need have anticipated no particular difficulty in obtaining the Pope's permission. But Katherine of Aragon was the aunt of Emperor Charles V, whose mother Juana the Mad had been her sister, and the Emperor Charles's vast territories included the northern Italian duchy of Milan and the southern Italian Kingdom of Naples. This made him a major force in Italian politics, whose wishes the Pope could hardly afford to ignore; and Charles, of course, was likely to object most strongly to any suggestion of repudiating his aunt. Moreover, Wolsey soon found that there was another obstacle in his way. He had intended to obtain the King's freedom from Katherine in order that Henry should immediately bind himself to the French cause, which Wolsey favoured, by marrying a princess of France; but he very quickly became unpleasantly aware that, in fact, Henry appeared to have no intention of marrying a princess from France or from anywhere else, since he had fallen besottedly in love with a certain Mistress Anne Boleyn.

Anne Boleyn was the daughter of a Kentish knight, Sir Thomas Boleyn, an extremely ambitious man who had made an advantageous marriage with the Duke of Norfolk's daughter, and who, in further pursuit of the advancement of his family, sent both Anne and her sister Mary abroad to receive an education and training at the courts of Margaret of Austria, Regent of the Netherlands, and of Claude of France, first wife of King Francis I. Although Claude herself was a model of propriety and decorum, Francis and his courtiers were notorious for their lax morals and for their pursuit of the ladies of the court; and very quickly rumour spread that none was easier to woo than Mary Boleyn. The King himself referred to her as his 'English mare' whom he had 'ridden' many times; and when it became known that other courtiers too had had similar success with her, Mary's position at court became untenable. At the prompting either of the

King himself or of her family, she was recalled to England in disgrace.

Her younger sister Anne, however, had no intention of making the same mistake. Although she rapidly became proficient in the art of flirting, which was so much practised at the French court, her reputation remained intact. She therefore stayed on at court, and thus she was able to be present in Queen Claude's entourage when Francis I and Henry VIII had their famous meeting at the Field of the Cloth of Gold, so called because of the extravagance with which the event was staged. Anne was probably only about 13 at the time (the date of her birth is not known for certain), and so is unlikely to have made much impression on Henry; but the Field of the Cloth of Gold did nevertheless play an important part in her life, for it was the failure of the two Kings to come to any lasting agreement there that led to war breaking out between England and France a year or so later. Since Anne was now a foreigner in an enemy country, her father at once recalled her home, and so she left the court of the French King and went, instead, to that of the English King.

Her future there promised well. Although she seems not to have been conventionally beautiful, there was a liveliness and vivacity about her which attracted men to her; and she had, moreover, the polish and sophistication which her years at the court of France had bestowed on her. Certainly she seems to have had no shortage of admirers. One was a near neighbour from Kent, Thomas Wyatt, later to become famous as a poet; he, however, was married already, although separated from his wife, and so nothing could come of it. Another of the young men who paid court to Anne did not suffer from this disadvantage, though, and was in all respects an eminently eligible suitor. This was Lord Henry Percy, heir to the earldom of Northumberland, a sensitive and delicate young man who seems to have offered Anne his wholehearted adoration. Anne seems to have returned his affection; moreover, marriage to him would, when his father died, make her a countess, which would please her ambitious family. The young couple found opportunities to meet on Sunday mornings, when Cardinal Wolsey, on whom Percy was attending, had a regular appointment with the

King. While King and cardinal were closeted together, the cardinal's attendants and the King's courtiers were at liberty, and Anne and Percy were able to pursue their courtship.

It did not, however, go unobserved. The court was a very public place; a romance between one of the Queen's ladies and one of the Cardinal's gentlemen was bound to be noticed and commented upon, and eventually word of it came to the ears of the King. Henry at once instructed Wolsey to make it quite clear to the young couple that there was no possibility of their relationship being allowed to continue. Their two families had already destined them to other partners: Anne to a young man named James Butler, in the hope that her marriage with him would settle a long-standing quarrel between his family and her own, and Lord Henry Percy to the Earl of Shrewsbury's daughter, Lady Mary Talbot. Neither of these marriage projects, Wolsey told the young man, could be set aside; in any case, he added, Lady Mary Talbot was, in terms of rank, a far more suitable bride for young Percy than Anne Boleyn, who, despite the fact that her mother was the Duke of Norfolk's sister, was too far below him in station. Percy tried to put up a resistance; but the Cardinal was all-powerful at court, and had also enlisted a powerful ally in the shape of the young man's formidable father the Earl of Northumberland, who had ridden post-haste from his northern estates to reprove his errant son. Forced to admit defeat, Percy was whisked back to the north for his marriage with Lady Mary Talbot, and Anne herself was sent back to her family's castle of Hever, deep in the countryside of Kent.

There she stayed for three years before being called back to court. This lengthy banishment seems to argue against any speculation that the reason the King had been so anxious for her not to marry Percy was that he himself was already attracted to her; it is, however, notable that although Percy's marriage with Lady Mary Talbot was immediately carried out, hers with James Butler was not, and indeed there appears to have been no further question of it. Perhaps her ambitious father had decided that if Anne could enchant the heir to an earldom, it might be worth holding out for a more splendid marriage for her than one with James Butler. It is also possible that Sir Thomas Boleyn's plans for this daughter were being further influenced by events in the career of his other daughter, Anne's sister Mary. For Mary, who had been brought home from France in disgrace for sleeping not only with King Francis but with his courtiers, was once again involved in an affair—this time with Henry VIII.

The family of a King's mistress could often expect considerable favours from the King. Mary Boleyn herself seems to have been an easy-going girl who made no particular attempt to procure any kind of advancement for herself; neither did the husband, William Carey, to whom for form's sake she had been married off. Her father, however, was another matter. Thomas Boleyn had always been eager to carve out a great position for himself and his family; now, with the King as his daughter's lover, he succeeded in getting himself raised to the peerage as Viscount Rochford, while his only son, George, was awarded lands and money. In this general bounty to the family Anne too was not forgotten; she was allowed to return to court.

Once again she was quick to attract admirers. Thomas Wyatt, her neighbour from Kent, who seems to have expressed interest in her when she first returned from France, was now in open pursuit of her, and Anne appears to have been not indifferent to him, for at one stage she bestowed on him a small jewelled pendant, which he wore concealed inside his clothes. Even had Wyatt not been already married, however, his chances of gaining Anne were slim, for very rapidly it became clear that she had another, and much more powerful, admirer. Henry VIII had tired of her sister Mary, and now turned his attentions to Anne.

Anne, however, had learned from the experiences of her sister, who had first been disgraced in France for sleeping with one King and who was now, despite the much improved position of her family, herself very little better off for sleeping with another. Anne had no intention of letting herself be bought as cheaply as Mary had been. Nor, however, could she openly rebuff the King. Instead she seems to have treated him much as she did her other suitors, and, as she had given Wyatt a jewelled pendant, so she now gave Henry a gold ring, which he wore on his little finger. On one occasion, when he and Wyatt were playing bowls and were unable to agree about a cast, Henry gestured at the bowl with the little finger so that Wyatt could plainly see Anne's token on it—only to be appalled when Wyatt, in turn, took out the pendant which Anne had given him and pretended to use the lace on which it hung to measure how far the bowl had travelled. Never in his life had Henry VIII been treated so by a woman. Furious, he kicked away the bowl and strode off from the game; but, contrary to the expectations of his courtiers, his anger was soon appeased, and his passion for Anne seemed, if anything, to be even more inflamed. Wyatt, however, soon took the opportunity to remove himself from the court by accompanying a friend on a diplomatic assignment to Italy, and ceased to play the dangerous game of rivalling his King in love.

The departure of Wyatt left the field clear for Henry, but for all that the King did not enjoy any greater degree of success with the elusive Anne Boleyn. In fact Anne's position was an extremely delicate one. The English court had no tradition of an established King's mistress. In France, in the preceding century, Charles VII's mistress Agnes Sorel had been installed almost as a second Queen, and Francis I bestowed similar position on his mistress Anne d'Heilly, Madame de Pisseleu; in England, by contrast, the previous King, Henry VIII's father Henry VII, had had no known mistresses at all, and Henry VIII himself had had his name publicly linked only with Elizabeth Blount and with Anne's own sister Mary. Neither of those had derived any great benefit from their association with the King. It was true that Elizabeth Blount's son by Henry had been created the Duke of Richmond, but she herself had never returned to court since his birth; and however well the rest of the Boleyn family had done out of Mary's affair with Henry, Mary and her husband were not substantially richer than they had been to start with. Anne, therefore, could see no great advancement to be gained from becoming Henry's mistress. On the other hand, Henry was all-powerful; and she and her family still had their way to make. Even if she did not wish to accept him, she certainly could not afford to incur his anger by finally refusing him. And meanwhile, she discovered that her reluctance to become his mistress was serving only to whet his appetite for her further, and to make his pursuit of her all the more pressing.

It was while matters stood like this that someone suggested the solution which would both free Henry from a wife who could not bear him sons and at the same time enable him to secure Anne Boleyn: a divorce from Katherine of Aragon. It is impossible to know for sure whose idea this was. Anne's enemies, and Katherine's friends, said that it was Anne herself, out of ambition and lust for power, who put the idea into Henry's head; Henry, on the other hand, claimed that it was suggested to him by a member of the French delegation which was in England in connection with the betrothal of the Princess Mary to the Dauphin. Certainly this was a time when Henry would have been particularly receptive to such a suggestion, since this marriage between the heirs to the thrones of France and England would have meant that, unless he produced a son, England would, after his death, become a possession of France. Marriage to a woman who could bear him a son would avoid that. And Anne's qualms about becoming his mistress would be irrelevant if she could become his wife instead.

Whether the idea appealed to Anne herself as much as it did to Henry, it is impossible to say. But even if it did not, there was no way for her to oppose it; and it would, after all, make her Queen of England, a position which could hardly have failed to hold some attraction for the daughter of an ambitious family. As for grounds for the divorce, it was not difficult to find some: before she married Henry, Katherine of Aragon had been the wife of his brother Arthur, and Henry, who fancied himself as something of a biblical scholar, was soon able to point to an injunction in the Bible that no man should marry his brother's widow. It was true that another part of the Bible seemed to have an exactly opposite meaning and to recommend that in fact a man *should* take to wife any woman whom the death of his brother left without a husband; Henry ignored that, since it did not suit his purposes. Instead, he appealed to the Pope for a divorce from Katherine on the grounds that, as the widow of his brother, she had never truly been his wife, and should instead be regarded only as the Dowager Princess of Wales.

The obvious person to carry such a request to the Pope was Cardinal Wolsey; but Wolsey would be only too well aware that his earlier interference in Anne's romance with Lord Henry Percy had made her his enemy, and that for Anne to become Queen would seriously endanger his own position, as well as making impossible the marriage with a French princess which he himself favoured. Wolsey, therefore, was kept in ignorance of the rôle of Anne, and was encouraged to think that the divorce which he was to request was to enable Henry to marry a Princess of France. Even had that been the case, however, he would have still found the Pope difficult to persuade; for Katherine of Aragon was the aunt of the Emperor Charles, and Charles was far too influential in Italian politics to be lightly offended. The best that Wolsey could achieve was that the case would be heard in England by himself and by a legate, Cardinal Campeggio, whom the Pope would send for the purpose. These were in fact stalling tactics: the Pope, at a loss which of the two sovereigns to offend, apparently hoped that by deferring the decision for as long as possible something might occur which would save him from the necessity of having to offend either.

A complicated pattern of motives and events was therefore set in motion. Of all the people involved, only Henry can certainly be said to have wanted the divorce to take place, as quickly as possible. Anne herself may or may not have done. Wolsey, when he eventually discovered that it would be Anne rather than a French princess who would be the new Queen, had certainly lost a good part of his reason for wanting to promote the divorce; but, on the other hand, the rise of Anne meant that he could definitely not afford to displease the King by hindering his will, and indeed might find his own position seriously undermined if he did not succeed in using his influence as a cardinal to procure the divorce. Campeggio certainly did not want to annoy the Emperor Charles by deciding the case against his aunt, but did not, if he could help it, wish to upset Henry either, and he and Wolsey therefore tried to bring about a compromise solution. Rather than letting the case actually come before the ecclesiastical court, they attempted to persuade Katherine of Aragon to do what, not many years before, Queen Jeanne of

France had been forced to do: to agree to the annulment of her marriage and to go into a convent.

Here, however, they came up against the one other fixed force in this web of imponderables: Katherine of Aragon herself. Just as Henry was irrevocably bent on divorce, so she was adamantly opposed to it, and her will was every bit as strong as his. She would never agree to the annulment of her marriage because to do so would be to call into question the legitimacy of her daughter Mary. She remained deaf to every appeal that could be made to her; she adamantly insisted that she herself was the rightful Queen and that Mary was the rightful heiress to the throne.

In the light of Katherine's refusal to compromise, Wolsey and Campeggio had no choice but to establish a court to decide the case. Evidence was taken from both sides. Katherine herself had always maintained that her marriage to Arthur had never been consummated; she continued to assert that now, and to declare that, in any case, a dispensation had been granted at the time of the marriage in which the Pope of the day had said that even had the marriage with Arthur been consummated her marriage with Henry would still be valid. Henry denied the existence of such a dispensation, and called witnesses who were prepared to swear that on the morning after the wedding Prince Arthur had told his attendants that he was exceptionally thirsty because he had spent the night 'in the midst of Spain', indicating that the marriage had indeed been consummated. He even descended to the unsavoury measure of having various of his courtiers relate their own early sexual adventures, which was intended to show that although Arthur was only 15 at the time of his death he was not too young to have been capable of intercourse.

All these efforts of the King's, however, still did not succeed in making Campeggio announce his decision. The legate's orders had been to play for time; this he did. And he acquired a still more powerful reason to do so when news came from Italy that the armies of Katherine's nephew the Emperor Charles, led by the French rebel the Duke of Bourbon, had stormed Rome, raping nuns, pillaging the inhabitants, and forcing the Pope himself to take refuge in the papal fortress, the Castel Sant'Angelo. This made the Pope effectively the Emperor's prisoner. He could certainly not afford to offend his powerful captor by agreeing to the divorce of his aunt.

On the other hand, there were also growing signs that it might not be advisable to upset Henry VIII either. Henry was not a patient man; he had expected a quick divorce and was rapidly growing very resentful of those he perceived as standing in the way of it. Foremost amongst these were Katherine of Aragon herself and their daughter, Mary; but Cardinal Wolsey, too, was beginning to fall out of favour as a result of his failure to expedite the divorce. To save himself, he offered to the King first his magnificent palace at Hampton Court, and then his London residence of Whitehall; but even gestures such as these could not shore up his crumbling power base. Those at court could clearly see that Wolsey's star was on the wane; and they could also use their own observation of Henry to tell them that he was a King who had little appetite for the day-to-day business of government and vastly preferred to delegate such details to a minister whom he could trust to see to them for him. Since the earliest days of the reign Wolsey had fulfilled this rôle; but now that the cardinal's fortunes were in decline, there was an opportunity for a new man to step forward and assume the position of the King's chief minister.

Such a man was Thomas Cromwell, of humble birth but able, energetic, ruthless, intelligent and, above all, able to suggest to Henry an idea that would not only provide a solution to the divorce problem but would also vastly increase the King's personal power and wealth. This was, quite simply, that Henry, instead of waiting and hoping for a decision from the Pope, should declare himself, the English church and England itself independent of papal authority. He could then establish a new English church with himself at the head, which would readily grant him his divorce, and he could also appropriate for himself the vast wealth and estates which had been accumulated by the Catholic church in England. If there was opposition to the idea from amongst his leading nobles—and the Tudors lived in perpetual fear of rebellion—then some of these plundered riches could be made over to them, in the form of money and lands. These would both act as bribes and also serve to give the ruling élite a vested interest in seeing that the old order was not restored, since if it were they themselves would stand to lose the pickings they had received from the dismemberment of the Roman church's power in England.

Cromwell's idea was not new: conflict between the Pope and temporal rulers went back at least as far as the Ghelf-Ghibelline struggles, and Henry VIII's older contemporary the Emperor Maximilian had dreamt of liberating himself from the shackles of papal authority by the simple expedient of being elected Pope himself, while in Sweden King Gustav Vasa was similarly enriching himself by dismantling the property and power of the church. Gustav Vasa, however, had also become a Protestant; and that was something that Henry VIII had no intention of doing. It was specifically Roman Catholicism, rather than Catholicism itself, which was to be the object of his campaign, and he envisaged himself being, as the Emperor Maximilian had hoped to become, a combination of monarch and Pope. Protestantism itself was a radical ideology with disturbing connotations of unsettling not only received ideas about religion but also the social fabric itself, and this was something that Henry VIII wanted no part of. Anne Boleyn herself appears to have been more favourably disposed towards the ideas of the Protestant reformers; indeed, during her years in France she had formed part of the Lutheran-influenced circle surrounding the French King's sister, Marguerite of Navarre the elder. But although it was in many ways for her sake that Henry VIII launched the English Reformation, it nevertheless tended to steer clear on the whole from issues of doctrine, and to concentrate much more on the wresting of power in the church out of the hands of the Pope and placing it firmly in those of the King.

This task was made all the easier by the fact that the Pope himself was still continuing his policy of attempting not to offend the King. He ignored all signs of what was coming; and he even agreed to appoint Henry's own nominee, Thomas Cranmer, to the vacant Archbishopric of Canterbury. No sooner had he done so than Cranmer declared the English church free of all bonds of allegiance to Rome, and further added that he himself would now decide the case of Henry's divorce from Katherine of Aragon. He immediately handed down judgement in Henry's favour, declared him a free man, and, shortly after, married him to Anne Boleyn.

Henry had had to wait a long time to achieve his desire; the delays of Campeggio and the appeals of Katherine had dragged the divorce process out for six long years. Throughout that time, however, he had shown no signs of swerving from his devotion to Anne. She herself had played her part admirably. At first she had kept the King's passion at blazing point by refusing to become his mistress; then, when the death of old Archbishop Wareham of Canterbury and the imminence of Cranmer's appointment meant that the end of the process was finally in sight, she played her trump card. First of all, she secured herself against possible disaster by persuading the King to create her Marquess of Pembroke in her own right, with the proviso that the title would descend not only to her legitimate heirs but also to any illegitimate ones. Having thus ensured that, even if she did not eventually become Queen, she and any children she might bear Henry would be provided for, she finally agreed to sleep with the King; and by the time she was crowned Queen, she was already pregnant with a child which, all the astrologers assured the delighted Henry, was, at long last, a male heir to the English crown.

Thus far Anne's career had progressed in a way that she could hardly have dreamed of. From being the younger daughter of a Kentish knight, she had risen to being Queen of England and, in all likelihood, the mother of its next King; the ambitious Sir Thomas Boleyn must have felt that his daughter had attained the very pinnacle of success. No sooner had she reached these dizzying heights, however, than her luck began to forsake her.

Anne's first misfortune was that her child, who was born four months after the coronation, was not a son but a daughter, christened Elizabeth after Henry's mother (this was also the name of his maternal grandmother, and of Anne's own mother too). Although this was a blow, it was not an insurmountable one, for she was still young and could have other children; but what was more serious still was that Henry was beginning to tire of her. The constancy which he had shown throughout their six years of courtship seemed to have evaporated as soon as he had finally got what he wanted. Perhaps as a result of Anne's pregnancy, or simply because the thrill of the chase was now over, Henry was soon rumoured to have turned to a new mistress, and when Anne reproached him with it he curtly informed her that she must 'put up with it as her betters had done'.

Anne, however, was hardly the woman to tolerate such a situation calmly. She made no secret of her resentment; indeed, she treated Henry in a way that at first simply astonished him, and then infuriated him. The rôle laid down for any sixteenth-century wife was to be meek, submissive, and obedient to her husband; Anne's behaviour, by contrast, was perceived as unruly, disorderly and deviant, and could even be likened to that most extreme form of female deviance, witchcraft. This was a suggestion fuelled by the fact that on one of her hands there was a rudimentary sixth finger, a congenital deformity which Anne always tried hard to conceal and which could, in contemporary terms, be interpreted as being one of the 'teats for the devil' which were supposed to be present on the bodies of witches. Since so many things, even moles, could be so interpreted, the presence of such a deformity would not in itself be likely to provoke any kind of accusation of witchcraft; but taken in conjunction with other things it could be dangerous. If, as has recently been suggested, Anne also miscarried of a deformed baby, she might well have been vulnerable to such a suggestion.

Even if the child of which she miscarried was not indeed deformed, the very fact that her pregnancy had not gone to term was already enough to put her position into jeopardy. Henry had certainly been in love with Anne when he married her, but love alone would not have been enough to elevate her to the position of Queen Consort; he had also been working on the presumption that she would be fertile. His nominal reason for divorcing Queen Katherine had been that her failure to bear sons must show that God was displeased by their marriage, and it was notable that his second marriage had not taken place until Anne was actually pregnant. But if Anne had achieved her position on the promise of her womb, that promise was to be lamentably unfulfilled. It was true that the baby Elizabeth was healthy enough; but after Elizabeth's birth, Anne's obstetric history proved scarcely less disastrous than that of her predecessor. Two or perhaps three pregnancies ended in miscarriage, and Henry VIII's volatile affections began to wander away from this Queen who had proved to be no better than his last one at giving him the longed-for son.

Anne's position was further worsened by developments on the political front. The fact that her marriage to Henry had displaced a Queen from Spain, the enemy of France, together with her upbringing in France and her personal acquaintance with Francis I, who had once been her sister's lover, meant that the French had, on the whole, adopted a relatively favourable attitude towards her marriage; but there was a limit to the goodwill they were prepared to show her. The blow fell when a message arrived requesting the fulfilment of an earlier treaty which had betrothed the Princess Mary to the Dauphin. If the French still recognized Mary as legitimate, then it meant that they regarded her, rather than Anne's own daughter Elizabeth, as the heiress of England; and Henry's dream of ensuring an undisputed succession was thus put in peril. Anne's own chance of regaining his favour was that she was now pregnant again; but then, once again, she miscarried, of a foetus which was apparently identifiable as male. When Henry was told, he stalked into her room and said: 'So you have lost my son; you get no more sons from me.' To Anne's protests he replied merely that he would speak to her when she was better.

True to his threat, Henry ceased to sleep with Anne after her final miscarriage, thus depriving her of any hope of ever bearing a son. He was already talking of finding a new wife. Anne's last remaining safeguard was, ironically enough, the fact that Katherine of Aragon was still alive; for as long as his first wife lived, Henry would not be able to repudiate Anne without being expected to take Katherine back. After she had been forcibly divorced, Katherine had been sent out of London and confined in what was considered to be the unhealthy climate of the area around Bedford and Huntingdon, where, it was hoped, she might well fall ill and die. Henry had even uttered direct threats of execution to both her and their daughter the Princess Mary; and it was widely considered that if he did not have them openly put to death, then Anne Boleyn might well do it covertly, by means of poison. Katherine, as befitted a daughter of Isabella the Catholic, had refused to succumb to either threat or persuasion to say anything to compromise either her own position or that of her daughter; but her health rapidly gave way beneath the strain. In January 1536 she died. She was buried on the same day that Anne Boleyn suffered her last miscarriage.

These two events sounded Anne's death knell. Now that Katherine was dead, Henry would be free to cast off Anne and marry a third time; and this time it would be a marriage of undoubted legitimacy, unlike that with Anne which could never be recognized by Catholics. The only obstacle in the way of this plan was Anne herself.

To that an answer was soon found. Thomas Cromwell, the man who had found his way into Henry's favour by showing him a way to free himself from his first wife, now saw an opportunity to strengthen his position still further by helping the King out of his second marriage too. Cromwell invited to dinner a young musician named Mark Smeaton, known to be a favourite of the Queen's. When Smeaton arrived Cromwell put him to the torture, using, amongst other techniques, a knotted rope twisted around the temples and tightened by being wound round a stick. Under such treatment Smeaton soon proved willing to confess to having had an affair with Anne; and adultery, in a Queen, was treasonable, and was punishable by death. For good measure, Cromwell decided to name various other young courtiers, in addition to Smeaton, as having been lovers of the Queen. All the charges were, in all probability, false—the evidence of Smeaton, being extracted from him under torture, need not be taken seriously—but they would still be fatal. In May 1536 first these young men, and then the Queen herself, were arrested.

The trial was of course a foregone conclusion; since the King obviously expected a verdict of guilty, that was what would be delivered, in spite of the fact that Anne's judges included her uncle, the Duke of Norfolk, and her first love Henry Percy, now the Earl of Northumberland. The main charge was adultery; but Cromwell was leaving no stone unturned in his quest to be rid of Anne forever, and he had decided not only to have the Queen accused of adultery, but also to get her marriage to Henry formally annulled, so that the little Elizabeth would no longer be in the succession to the crown. The grounds for this were to be that Anne had been pre-contracted to the Earl of Northumberland and had therefore been unable to contract any subsequent marriage while the Earl was still alive. This, however, led to a complication: if Anne had never legally been Henry's wife, it was hardly logical to accuse her of adultery against him. It was perhaps to obviate this potential problem that Cromwell entered another charge in the indictment: he accused Anne of having committed incest with her own brother George, Lord Rochford—something which would remain a crime whether she were the King's wife or not.

Anne's doom was sealed. Only one mercy was to be allowed her: instead of the ghastly death by burning to which she might have been condemned, she would not even have to risk the headsman's axe—which could sometimes botch the job badly—but would be dispatched by the sharp sword of an executioner specially imported from Calais for the purpose. The only other thing in which she could take comfort, she told her ladies, was that she was innocent of all the crimes she was accused of, and guilty only of having wished for the death of the Princess Mary. She divided her time between praying for forgiveness and bouts of hysterical laughter, until on the morning of 19 May 1536, on Tower Green, Anne, Queen of England, knelt on the block in front of the assembled dignitaries, and stretched out her neck for the sword of the executioner from Calais.

To Anne Boleyn there had thus fallen the unenviable distinction of becoming the first Queen to be judicially put to death. Her successor, however, was more fortunate. Henry had already selected Jane Seymour as his third wife before the death of his second; and part of what attracted him to her may well have been that she seems to have been everything that Anne was not—shy, modest, unassuming, plain and gentle, and, unlike Anne, whose own ancestry was unimpressive, able to claim descent from Edward III. Like Anne, however, she had ambitious relatives—in her case, her brothers Edward and Thomas Seymour—and, whether coached by them of her own accord, she too, like Anne, refused any suggestion of becoming merely the King's mistress when it seemed as though she could perhaps become his wife instead. She returned to him a purse of gold which he had sent her, and refused to receive him except in the presence of her brother and sister-in-law. Her modest and virtuous behaviour presented a sharp contrast to the hysterics and furies to which Anne had become prone, and the King was enchanted with her. On the very day that Anne was executed he contracted a betrothal with her; ten days after that, he married her.

As in the case of Anne Boleyn, Henry's initial ardour appears to have undergone a cooling-off after marriage. Although Jane did succeed in effecting a reconciliation between him and the Princess Mary, she irritated him by her preference for pre-Reformation ways, and sometimes found herself on the receiving end of his formidable temper. Jane, however, soon developed a foolproof method of protection, by becoming pregnant. And when her child was born, Henry VIII's greatest dream was finally realized: he had a son.

Jane, however, had been greatly weakened by the birth, and soon afterwards developed puerperal fever. Nine days after the birth of the little Prince Edward, she died.

Henry VIII was genuinely grief-stricken by her death. He made arrangements to be buried by her side in the chapel at Windsor Castle, and for a while he would not hear any talk of marrying again. But although the baby Edward seemed healthy, one son was hardly enough to secure the succession, and now that his first three wives were all dead there was no legal impediment to Henry contracting a fourth marriage. Moreover, the political situation had changed for the worse. The thing that Henry had dreaded for many years had finally taken place: the Emperor Charles V and the King of France had at last agreed to patch up their differences and were now united in a common front against England. Henry desperately needed allies; and since his breach with Rome meant that he would not find any amongst Catholic potentates, he would have to look to the Protestant princes of Germany to supply them.

This was a proposition that he found deeply unattractive.

He had a considerable dislike of the more radical elements of Protestantism, and he was also very anxious about having to commit himself to a bride whom he had never seen. Although this was a relatively common experience for Kings and princes, it would be a new one for Henry: Katherine of Aragon had been living in England when he married her, and Anne Boleyn and Jane Seymour had both been at his court. He had developed a horror of saddling himself with a bride who might prove to be unattractive, and before his breach with Francis I he had even made the startling suggestion that Francis might like to line up a few of the prettiest French princesses at Calais for him to be able to inspect them. Now, however, he would have to confine himself to the secondhand evidence of such pictures as his painter, Hans Holbein, could manage to produce of prospective brides.

The princess who was eventually successful in this beauty contest of portraits was Anne of Cleves, whose brother the Duke of Cleves could provide Henry with his much-needed ally on the Continent. The Cleves marriage was very actively encouraged by Thomas Cromwell, who wanted to ensure the continuing success of the English Reformation which he had helped Henry to launch; and the continuing alliance between France and the Emperor gave Henry little choice but to go through with it. So despite his reservations about marrying a woman whom he had been unable to see for himself, treaties were duly drawn up and Anne of Cleves arrived in England to become the fourth wife of Henry VIII.

Henry's first sight of his new bride confirmed all his worst fears. Anne seems to have been heavily-built—something which would not have been apparent to Henry from the Holbein portrait of her, which showed only her head and bust—and had also suffered from smallpox, which, it appears, had left its marks plainly on her face. What was calculated to displease Henry at least as much as these physical defects was that she spoke almost no English, and indeed seemed altogether lacking in accomplishments of any sort: her table manners were not those to which the English court was accustomed, and she was completely ignorant of music, which was Henry's great delight. Henry swore to his councillors that he would not be going through with the marriage at all except for the good of his realm; and even when the marriage had actually been solemnized, he told them the next morning that the sight of her had so sickened him that he had been quite unable to consummate it. This was also, of course, good policy on Henry's part: for if the marriage were not consummated, then it would always be possible for him to get it annulled. And, quite apart from the King's dislike for his wife, there were two other good reasons why this should happen: the breakdown of the alliance between France and Spain, which rendered the Cleves alliance politically redundant, and the fact that Henry's eye had been caught by a pretty young maid-in-waiting to the Queen, named Catherine Howard.

Given the chequered matrimonial history of Henry VIII, it was hardly surprising that Anne of Cleves should soon suspect what was in the air. When the King had still been casting around for a fourth wife, Christina, the widowed Duchess of Milan, had replied to his proposal that she would only have married him if she had had an extra head to lose; and now Anne of Cleves began to fear that she would go the same way as Anne Boleyn had done. At first she behaved irritably, until Cromwell, desperate to preserve the marriage on which he had staked his career, sent her a message begging her to try to make herself more agreeable to the King; Anne took him literally and nearly drove Henry mad by constantly clinging to and fawning on him. But her fears were needless. Although her brother's friendship might no longer be so urgently required by Henry, the Duke of Cleves was still too important a person to upset more than was needful. As he had done with Katherine of Aragon, Henry offered Anne a compromise: if she would agree to the annulment of her marriage, she could live respected in England with the honorary title of 'King's sister'. And unlike Katherine of Aragon, Anne, who of course had no children to fight for, readily agreed to this proposal. So delighted was the King at his release that he showered her with gifts and goodwill; and indeed Anne herself seemed scarcely less pleased to have emerged so well from a difficult situation. The French ambassador reported that she was 'more joyous than ever, and wears new dresses every day'. She even refused the request of her brother that she should return to Cleves, where she could be used in another diplomatic marriage; she had not found the delights of Queenship so sweet that she was eager to sample them again, and instead she proved perfectly willing to remain in England for the rest of her life, living exactly as she pleased, converting to Catholicism—which she could never have done in the Lutheran duchy of her brother—and remaining on good terms with everyone, even with her own successor, the King's fifth wife Catherine Howard.

The King had married Catherine soon after his divorce from Anne, to the immense delight of the Catholic party. Anne's fall had brought with it the downfall of Thomas Cromwell, who, shortly after his promotion to the Earldom of Essex, had been accused of treason and executed; and with him had gone his actively pro-Reformation policy. Whereas Anne of Cleves had been the sister of a Lutheran duke, Catherine Howard was a scion of the staunchly Catholic Howard family. She was also, by coincidence, a first cousin of Anne Boleyn, whose mother Elizabeth Howard had been a sister of Catherine's father Lord Edmund Howard. Although she had probably never met Anne, this close kinship led Queen Catherine to show particular favour to her cousin's little daughter the Princess Elizabeth, whose life had been a sad one since the death of her mother; but in other respects, her behaviour was soon to show that she had learned little from the tragic career of her cousin and predecessor.

Catherine had been brought up at Lambeth, in the household of her step-grandmother the Dowager Duchess of Norfolk. Nominally the old lady was supposed to provide supervision for the numerous brood of Howard daughters, nieces and cousins growing up under her roof; in practice, it seemed that the girls did exactly what they liked—and what they liked was the company of young men. Long before she ever met Henry Catherine had entangled herself with two separate youths in her grandmother's household; one, a musician named Mannox, who had given her music lessons and had apparently been allowed by Catherine to indulge in some fairly heavy petting with her, and another, Francis Dereham, who had apparently been engaged to her and had been in the habit of visiting her bed in the girls' dormitory at Lambeth on a nightly basis.

All this had taken place when Catherine was very young, and perhaps if she had been discreet it would all have remained unknown and she could have continued to enjoy her position as the adored, spoilt young bride of an ageing and ailing King. But Catherine was not discreet. Henry by now was no longer the handsome young man who had married Katherine of Aragon; he was grossly overweight, he was already suffering from a suppurating ulcer on one leg, and it has also been suggested that he was afflicted by a variety of other conditions from scurvy to syphilis. The fact that none of his wives after Jane Seymour conceived a child by him suggests that he may have been impotent, or at least infertile; he was certainly not, in any sense of the word, desirable. Catherine, with her nightly romps with Dereham, was used to a more exciting life than that which could be offered by her ageing husband, and she was determined to have it. Although she had tired of Dereham himself, she took as her lover her cousin, Thomas Culpeper. When she went on a progress to the north with the King Culpeper came too, and at their nightly stops would sneak up the back stairs to the Queen's apartment.

Such dangerous dealing was almost bound to be found out sooner or later. What seems to have emerged first was the history of Catherine's life in the household of the Dowager Duchess of Norfolk, which came out through a 'discontented former servant of the old duchess'. Since all this had happened before Catherine had even met the King, Henry, when told, was not particularly indignant; but he did order enquiries to be made, and the information that was revealed by them devastated him. Henry, who had already dragged the sexual reputations of two of his wives before public tribunals by accusing Katherine of Aragon of having falsely claimed to be a virgin and Anne Boleyn of mass adultery, now found himself proclaimed a cuckold indeed. He was at Hampton Court when the news was brought to him. He wept in front of his embarrassed councillors, and then left at once for London, leaving the matter in the hands of the Council. Hearing of his departure and of the accusations that had been made against her, Catherine begged to be allowed an audience with him; but the King was adamant. He would have nothing more to do with the woman he had once called his 'rose without a thorn'.

She could still, perhaps, have saved herself. If she had claimed to be pre-contracted to Culpeper, then she would, legally, never have been the wife of the King at all; and therefore she could not be accused of adultery against him, and might hope to suffer a lesser punishment than death. But this was a solution that Catherine adamantly refused. She stuck firm in her assertion that there had been no pre-contract, and was accordingly found guilty of adultery and treason. Whether she was aware of it or not, she had, by this clinging to the title of Queen, effectively signed her own death-warrant. Like Queen Anne Boleyn before her she was sent to the Tower, where she talked much of the cousin who had shared with her the twin fates of Queenship and of death; and when, on a cold February day, she was led out to her execution, the scaffold was erected on the spot where Anne had died, and her body was afterwards buried close to Anne's. According to one report, her last words were 'I die a Queen, but I would rather have died the wife of Culpeper'; but it is also possible to see her adamant refusal to admit to any pre-contract with Culpeper as a determination that she was prepared to pay the price of death if she died with her title of Queen.

The last wife of Henry VIII was very different from her predecessor. Katherine Parr was, at the age of 31, already twice widowed; she had spent much of her life so far caring for elderly husbands, and it seems now that she was free for the second time she had a mind to please herself in her third marriage, by accepting the proposal which Thomas Seymour, brother of the dead Queen Jane Seymour, seemed likely to make to her. When she attracted the attention of Henry VIII, however, all prospect of such a marriage disappeared. Katherine might be much less than eager for Queenship; but it was not a title that could be refused. Seymour discreetly removed himself from the scene and Katherine Parr, formerly Lady Latimer, became Queen of England as the sixth wife of Henry VIII.

Katherine was a sensible, intelligent woman with strong intellectual interests, who immediately proceeded to concern herself actively and affectionately with the education of her three step-children, Mary, who was about Katherine's age and was already a close friend of hers, Elizabeth and Edward. Like Jane Seymour's, her family, the Parrs of Kendal, could claim royal descent, and the practice in nursing which Katherine had obtained from her two previous marriages to elderly husbands further fitted her as a consort to the King. Some aspects of his new wife's character, however, Henry found less congenial. In particular, he disliked her strong inclination towards Protestantism, and indeed seems to have resented the fact that she should even hold religious opinions independently from his own. This was a potential cause for discord that was soon seized upon by those favourers of the Old Religion who disliked seeing a Queen with Protestant leanings, and on one occasion when Katherine had clung forcefully to her own opinion in discussion with Henry they seem even to have persuaded him to agree to her arrest and interrogation. Possibly at the instigation of the King, however, Katherine got to learn of her impending danger, and cried so loudly that Henry sent to know what was the matter. She at once told him that she had not meant to maintain an opinion different from his but had merely been seeking guidance from him; Henry promptly forgave her, and when her enemies arrived the next day to arrest her he soundly berated them. It is indeed possible that much of the episode had been engineered by him as a warning to her, and certainly there was no interruption to their relationship after that. The brief period of rumours of a possible seventh wife died down, and Katherine remained as Queen of England until the death of Henry VIII in January 1547 finally put an end to his troubled marital career.

Katherine herself, however, had not finished with marriage. Although she had already survived three husbands, she was still eager for a fourth: Thomas Seymour, who had already courted her once before the intervention of Henry VIII had put a stop to it. Now that Henry was dead, the new King was his only son Edward VI, a child of 10. The youth of the King meant that a regency or protectorate would be necessary, and the two most obvious contenders to fill this powerful position would be the young King's two maternal uncles, Thomas Seymour himself and his elder brother, Edward. Seniority of years would automatically give Edward the advantage; but the ambitious Thomas may well have seen marriage to the Dowager Queen—who could indeed have been a possible candidate for the Regency in her own right, since she had already exercised it when Henry VIII was in France—as boosting his own chances of obtaining power. In the event, Thomas miscalculated; although the young King Edward was very fond of his stepmother, Queen Katherine's second marriage was easily used by her political adversaries to disgrace her at court, since she had not asked permission before contracting it. The position of Lord Protector went to Edward Seymour, who was also created Duke of Somerset, and a war for precedence at court promptly broke out between Edward's wife, the new Duchess of Somerset, and Katherine Parr, which led to considerable ill-feeling between the brothers.

Although Thomas Seymour might have lost a battle, however, he had by no means lost the war. There were still various expedients he could try in his quest for power, and the first and most daring of these might well be to get his new wife pregnant. Some time before his death Henry VIII had changed his will, to give any children he might have by Katherine Parr precedence in the succession over Mary and Elizabeth; and if Katherine were to produce a child rapidly enough after Henry's death, it might well be possible for Thomas to pass it off as the old King's and thus as the rightful heir to the crown if King Edward died without issue. Although the Queen did indeed become pregnant, however, it was not until after too long a period had elapsed since Henry's death for there to be any chance of claiming the child as his. So Thomas turned his attention to another possible line of attack.

Katherine Parr had grave fears that her pregnancy might cost her her life, and since she was by now well into her thirties, an advanced age for a first baby in Tudor times, there was a strong possibility that her forebodings might be justified. In that case, Thomas Seymour would be free to marry again; and there could be few more eligible brides than the young Princess Elizabeth herself, whose Protestantism had made her a favourite with her brother King Edward VI, and who was in fact living with Queen Katherine and Seymour at the time. Seymour seems to have set about the business of paying court to Elizabeth, very possibly with the intention of trying to make her his wife if Katherine Parr were to die in childbirth; but although the 13-year-old Elizabeth seems to have been unaware of quite what he was doing or what it might lead to, Katherine Parr was not so innocent. Catching her husband engaged in boisterous horseplay with the princess, she seems to have guessed at once at what was afoot, and had Elizabeth sent away. Soon afterwards, however, the Queen, as she had feared, was brought to bed of a daughter, failed to recover from the birth, and died of puerperal fever. The child was christened Mary, perhaps after Katherine's great friend the Princess Mary, and seems to have been sent to the house of the Dowager Duchess of Suffolk, a friend of her late mother; but since nothing is known of what became of her afterwards, it is usually assumed that she died in childhood. It has been claimed that she married a Sir Edward Bushell and had children, but this has never been proved; so obscurity engulfs the fate of the little girl who, daughter of one Queen and stepsister of two others, might even have sat on a throne itself if she had been born soon enough after the death of Henry VIII to be passed off as his.

The fact that Henry VIII's own matrimonial career had been so tumultuous did not stop him from adopting a distinctly censorious attitude towards the exploits of his older sister, Margaret, Queen of Scotland. Margaret's life was not a happy one. Unlike her younger sister Mary, their parents' and their brother's favourite, Margaret was not beautiful; but as the elder of the two daughters of Henry VII, it was she who was chosen to cement the vital alliance between England and its northern neighbour by a marriage with King James IV of Scotland. Negotiations for the marriage began in 1495 but proved so problematic that they were not completed until 1503, and even then it was decided that, since Margaret was still only 13, she should not travel to Scotland till the following year. During this period of waiting Margaret lost her mother,

Elizabeth of York; and she scarcely had time to recover from this before she found herself, still a young, inexperienced girl, travelling to the bleak north to face a much older husband and the hideously complicated political situation of Scotland.

From the earliest days of her marriage Margaret was constantly writing home, first to her father King Henry VII and then to his successor, her brother King Henry VIII, asking them for advice, help and sympathy. She missed her home, her husband was constantly unfaithful to her, and the marriage was not helped by the fact that it failed, at first, to produce healthy children. Two sons and a daughter did not survive infancy, and Margaret also found that pregnancies made her very ill and left her needing months to recover from them—almost certainly because she suffered from the heritable disease porphyria, of which so many of her descendants were later to show symptoms. Finally, however, a son, James, was born to the Queen, and lived; but when he was only a year old Margaret's husband James IV decided to respond to a plea for help from the French Queen, Anne of Brittany, by resurrecting the 'auld alliance' between France and Scotland. He hoped to take advantage of the fact that Margaret's brother Henry VIII was campaigning in France; but Henry's first wife Katherine of Aragon proved herself more than equal to the task of sending an army to tackle the Scottish attack. The Scottish forces were annihilated and the King himself was killed, leaving Margaret Tudor a widow of 23, four months pregnant and with a baby son to protect. Margaret knew that she had to act fast. Fearing that as her pregnancy advanced she would once again become incapacitated by illness, she immediately had her son crowned King; for once, however, her pregnancy was trouble-free, and early the next year she gave birth to another son, thus bolstering both the succession to the crown and her own standing.

Margaret, however, seems to have felt that she could no longer maintain her position single-handed. Three months after the birth of her son, she secretly married the 19-year-old Earl of Angus.

Margaret appears to have been deeply in love with Angus, but the Scottish nobles were by no means so enthusiastic. By remarrying, they argued, the widowed Queen had forfeited her claim to the Regency; fighting broke out between her supporters and theirs, and the two princes were kidnapped by the nobles. Margaret, who was by now pregnant again, had no choice but to flee with Angus to England, where her daughter Margaret was born at Morpeth Castle after a labour of great length and difficulty. There two disasters fell on her in rapid succession: the news that her younger son had died while in the care of the nobles, and the fact that her young husband the Earl of Angus rapidly tired of a sick and unsuccessful Queen and returned to Scotland, where he reached a separate peace with the nobles. Margaret did, however, receive a message from her brother Henry VIII saying that he would receive her, so, taking her little daughter Margaret with her, she travelled south and was reunited with both her brother and her sister Mary, now returned from her own brief career as Queen of France and installed as the wife of her beloved Charles Brandon.

Margaret's period of happiness and respite was short. Persuaded by her brother, she agreed to a reconciliation with Angus and returned to Scotland, after the nobles had agreed to her return on the condition that she behave like 'ane guid Scottis woman'. This, however, she did not do. Disgusted by her husband's infidelity, she succeeded in obtaining from the Pope a divorce from him, and proceeded to marry for a third time, this time to Henry Stewart of Methven, a much less important noble than Angus but one whom she found more congenial. Despite the fact that Henry VIII himself was to divorce not one spouse but three (counting the annulment of his marriage to Anne Boleyn), he never forgave his sister for what he saw as her inexcusably wanton behaviour. They remained estranged until her death in 1541, and when he drew up his will he specifically excluded Margaret's descendants from the succession on the grounds that they were 'foreign'. His attempt to keep the Scottish line from the throne was to be unsuccessful, however. Ninety-nine years after Margaret had travelled south to be married, her great-grandson, James VI of Scotland, was declared James I of England by right of his descent from her, and thus united the two crowns.

Part II:

Women Rulers

V

Female Regents

ALTHOUGH the great majority of women in the sixteenth century found that the only kind of power they were able to exercise at all was through men, there were some who were able to attain for themselves a status in their own right. One condition that was particularly favourable for this purpose was that of widowhood; once a woman had passed from the authority both of her father and of her husband, she often found that she was able to achieve at least a limited form of independence. The widows of tradesmen and merchants would, if they did not have an adult son or son-in-law, often inherit their husband's property and clientele, and might thus find themselves able to take their pick of a second husband from amongst a host of ambitious young men who saw marriage to a widow as a rapid and profitable way of rising in the world; similarly, the widow of a King who had not left an adult make heir might well find herself able to exercise authority during the minority of the new ruler. During the sixteenth century, Queen Margaret Tudor and Queen Mary of Guise in Scotland and Queen Catherine de' Medici in France all found themselves in this position, and all, with varying degrees of success, attempted to rule as Regents. There were also a small group of women who, without possessing the actual title of Queen, nevertheless managed to exercise an authority normally reserved only for a King. In France, Louise of Savoy, the mother of Francis I, was Regent for her son during his Italian wars and the captivity in Spain which followed them; while in the Netherlands, the concentration of so many geographically dispersed territories in the hands of Charles V and Philip II of Spain meant that both Kings turned to female members of their families to rule as their deputies in the war-torn provinces of the Low Countries to which they themselves were able to travel only infrequently.

There was, however, a considerable difference between the Regencies of Margaret Tudor, Mary of Guise and Catherine de' Medici, and those of Louise of Savoy and the Governors of the Netherlands. The Netherlands had passed to the Spanish Kings by a historical accident—the marriage of Juana of Castile to the Archduke Philip, who had inherited the Low Countries from his mother Mary of Burgundy—and there was a strong feeling that the allegiance the provinces owed was not to the Spanish crown as such, but merely to their own Duke, who simply happened to be King of Spain as well. For this reason, and given the fact that during the course of the century the political and religious troubles in the Netherlands became ever more severe, it was highly inadvisable to send a Spanish grandee, who would automatically be seen as an alien, to govern them. Charles V and Philip II were therefore obliged to use as Regents of the Netherlands members of their own family, who, like themselves, shared the ducal blood of Burgundy. Both Kings, however, suffered a distinct shortage of male adult relatives who would be suitable for this purpose; and both, therefore, fell back on female relations in the absence of male ones.

But if the authority of the female Governors of the Netherlands was based largely on the fact that they were members of the indigenous ruling family, the situation was very different for Margaret Tudor, Mary of Guise and Catherine de' Medici. For each of these women suffered the consequences of the tradition that a King should make a dynastic alliance by a marriage with a princess from another country; each of them was a foreigner in the country which they were trying to govern, and each of them was, therefore, resented by the native nobility over which they tried to exercise their authority.

When Margaret Tudor returned from her brief sojourn at the court of her brother Henry VIII, the Duke of Albany, whom the Scottish nobles had appointed as Regent in Margaret's absence, said that he would only have her back in Scotland if she would promise to behave herself like 'ane guid Scottis woman'. As a matter of fact Albany was hardly more Scots than Margaret herself was, having spent all his adult life in France; but France was at least the traditional ally of Scotland, whereas Margaret was a princess from England, Scotland's age-long enemy. It had been the armies of Margaret's brother Henry VIII of England which had defeated and killed the Scots King in battle, and Henry's sister was consequently seen as a very dangerous person to have as Regent. Margaret had, of course, attempted to buy herself local allies and a purchase amongst the native Scottish nobility by her marriage with one of their number, the young Earl of Angus, but this had served little purpose other than to generate jealousy and rivalry, and in any case the fact that the marriage was a disaster served to negate any useful effect it might ever have had. In the end Margaret found it impossible to stamp her authority on the Scots nobles and was forced effectively to withdraw from political life.

Mary of Guise met with rather more success. Although his mother was English, Margaret Tudor's son James V was determined to cement the traditional alliance of Scotland and France by taking to wife a French princess. His first attempt to do this ended in failure when his bride, the Princess Madeleine, sickened and died in the rigours of the Scottish climate after only two months of marriage; and perhaps because of this, he chose as a second wife a much more robust woman, Mary of Guise-Lorraine, whom he had already seen and admired on a visit to France. Mary's family were already rapidly gaining ascendancy in French politics, and since she herself was already a widow with a small son, she was clearly capable of bearing male children.

Despite this promising start, however, the marriage was not, at first, a particular success. James V was a complicated man; he almost certainly suffered from the porphyria which had been transmitted to him by his mother Margaret Tudor—and which was later to take such devastating form in his descendant King George III—and he was prey to violent changes of mood and black depressions. He was a frenetic womanizer, and since his expeditions in search of new conquests often took him out to the countryside amongst the common people, he acquired something of a reputation as 'The Poor Man's King'; but he was also capable of cruelty and of treachery, and when two sons that had been born to him and Mary died as babies, it was said that the sins of the father were being visited on the children. Mary, however, despite a series of bad colds, soon became pregnant again, and in December 1542 she gave birth to a daughter, christened Mary after her mother. The news of the child's birth, however, brought no comfort to James V. Two weeks earlier, the Scots had been beaten at the hands of the English at the battle of Solway Moss. At the news of the defeat, James appeared to lose the will to live. He took to his bed, and when told of the birth of his daughter, said merely, 'It came with a lass; it will go with a lass'—referring to the fact that the crown had come to the Stewarts through a woman, Robert the Bruce's daughter Marjorie, and, interestingly, correctly predicting the eventual end of the line in the person of Queen Anne. Then he turned his face to the wall and died, at the age of only 30, leaving his six-days-old daughter as Queen in his stead, and Scotland a prey to the English invaders.

Mary of Guise, however, was not so easily beaten as her husband had been. Although she was unable to obtain the Regency, which went instead to the Earl of Arran, she kept her head amongst the tortuous twists and turns of Scottish politics. She resisted the suggestion that the little Queen should be given in marriage to Prince Edward, the heir to the English throne, and eventually saw her own wishes fulfilled when her daughter, now aged 5, was sent to the safety of Mary's own native France, where Mary's Guise-Lorraine relatives could keep a watchful eye on her and where, one day, a glorious future awaited her: she had been betrothed to the Dauphin Francis, which meant that she would, one day, be Queen of France, in addition to her own inheritance of Scotland. In the meantime, however, there was much hard work to be done to protect that inheritance; and since the little Queen of Scots was both too young and too far away to be able to do anything about it, her mother would have to do it instead.

The task facing Mary of Guise was a difficult one. Not only was she a foreign Queen in a country without an adult ruler and threatened by its belligerent neighbour Henry VIII of England; she also had to contend with the growing agitation for religious reform in Scotland. Whereas reform of the Catholic church had to a large extent been imposed from above in England by Henry VIII, in Scotland there was genuine and widespread popular support for it—a fact which was all the harder for Mary to cope with since she was herself a devout Catholic. An early blow struck by the Reformers was the murder of Cardinal Beaton, who had been a staunch personal and political supporter of Mary, and whose death was therefore a great loss to her. It may, indeed, have been partly the murder of Cardinal Beaton which finally decided Mary of Guise to send her little daughter to France, where at least she would be safe; but however satisfactory it was in personal terms for her to betroth her daughter to the son of the King of France, it was a decision which brought with it considerable political problems. France was a Catholic country, and so the young Mary, Queen of Scots, would be brought up as a Catholic, despite the fact that her own Scottish subjects were moving daily nearer to Protestantism; and even more serious was the fact that the young Queen of Scots' marriage to the future French King would turn Scotland into a virtual province of France. Even if the Scottish nobles proved prepared to tolerate such a situation, the country could never again expect to reap the benefits of strong personal government by a ruler who was on the spot; it would instead be governed by an absentee Queen who knew little of her subjects, was not even of the same religion as they, and was expected to combine the two very different functions of being a Queen Regnant in one country and a Queen Consort in another.

Some of the dangers inherent in the situation became apparent when Mary of Guise decided, despite the turbulent situation at home, to make a visit to France, both to see her children—her son from her first marriage as well as the little Mary, Queen of Scots—and also to ask for political and financial assistance from the French King. It must certainly have been a pleasure to her to see her little daughter once again; but otherwise the visit was not a successful one, for during the course of it Mary's son from her first marriage fell ill and died, and she also failed to secure the help she wanted from Henry II of France. Even more ominously, news came from Scotland that Lord James Stewart, a bastard son of James V and thus a half-brother to the young Queen of Scots, had taken advantage of the absence of the Regent to make his own bid for power, and had already established friendly relations with both England and the Scottish Reformers. It was a warning sign that Scotland was too tempestuous a country to be successfully governed from a distance, and Mary of Guise accordingly set out on her travels again, journeying first to England, where she too attempted to win the confidence of the young Edward VI and his advisers, and then to Scotland to resume the Regency which it was clearly so dangerous to abandon.

So while her daughter continued happily in France, winning praise from all quarters for her beauty and charm, Mary of Guise returned to attempt to keep Scotland peaceful, orderly, and Catholic. During her absence, however, the nobles sympathetic to reform had been able to gain considerable ground, and they also benefited from a change of ruler in England, where the Catholic Mary Tudor was succeeded by her Protestant half-sister Elizabeth. Elizabeth, who hated war, was not prepared to intervene openly in the affairs of Scotland, but she was certainly willing to give the Protestant lords all the assistance she could in secret. Mary of Guise, on the other hand, had only France to turn to. By this time her daughter Mary, Queen of Scots, had married the Dauphin Francis, and the French did, therefore, give her help, but there was a limit to what they could do, and Mary of Guise was forced to rely for the most part on her own native wits and courage.

Her position was doubly difficult because she was a woman. The Scottish reformer John Knox had recently published his *First Blast of the Trumpet Against the Monstrous Regiment of Women*: 'regiment', in this sense, meant rule, and Knox's argument was that women were by their very sex and nature unfit for government, which should be vested only in the hands of men. A principal factor which had induced Knox to write this was the fact that, by coincidence, both England and Scotland were at the time being ruled by women—England by Mary Tudor and Scotland by Mary of Guise—and both of these Queens were Catholic, and hence anathema to Knox. When Catherine de' Medici came to power in France as Regent for her son Charles IX, French Protestant Reformers would produce similar arguments about the inadmissibility and illegality of all feminine rule. Knox himself, however, found himself severely embarrassed by his own arguments when Mary Tudor died and was succeeded by her sister Elizabeth—also a Queen, but this time a Protestant one—and found himself having to do quite a bit of humiliating back-tracking to appease the new Queen, who made her dislike for his arguments very clear. But although he declared that Elizabeth herself was that rarity, a Queen whose rule was sanctioned by God, he did not relent in the case of Mary of Guise, and even went so far as to accuse the Scottish Queen Regent, whose reputation was otherwise entirely blameless, of sexual incontinence, declaring that Cardinal Beaton and various other Catholic dignitaries had all been her lovers.

In addition to the fact of her sex, which made her vulnerable to such slurs, Mary of Guise was also having to contend with increasing ill-health. She suffered from the painful disease of dropsy, which caused swelling, and complained that her legs were 'as soft as butter' because of it. Her troubles came to a head when in 1560, two years after she had come to the throne of England, Elizabeth I finally agreed to give open support to the Protestant nobles and declared war on Scotland. Mary of Guise was forced to take refuge in Edinburgh Castle, and there, worn out by the troubles of her administration and desperately ill from dropsy, she died. Her spirit and courage did not falter to the last, and even won admiration from the Protestant lords; she asked them to pardon 'what she had done amiss' and movingly pleaded with them to return to their allegiance to her daughter. They did, however, insist that she should see a Protestant pastor, and this the dying Queen was forced to comply with. Her last wish had been to die in France, close to her family and her daughter, and in order for her to do this her younger brother had already set sail for Scotland so that he could take over the Regency while she returned to France; but by the time he arrived, to relieve her of the burden which she had carried for so long, Mary of Guise had already breathed her last.

Scarcely had the Scottish Queen Regent disappeared from the international political scene when a French one took her place. Mary of Guise's daughter Mary, Queen of Scots, was now Queen of France as well; but she had barely recovered from hearing of the death of her mother when her husband, too, fell ill and died, at the age of only 17. His successor was his younger brother, Charles IX; but since the new king was only 10 years old, the real power passed at once into the hands of his mother, Catherine de' Medici.

Catherine had suffered many long years of neglect and insult, for which she was now able to be revenged. Her late husband's mistress, Diane de Poitiers, was forced to return the jewels and châteaux which the King had showered on her, and Catherine's widowed daughter-in-law Mary, Queen of Scots was packed off home to Scotland. For the first time since she had come to France, the Queen Mother reigned supreme at her own court.

But although Catherine had rid her court of two beautiful women, Diane de Poitiers and Mary, Queen of Scots, she was by no means averse to having beauty around her in general. Indeed, although it was something she had never possessed herself, she was very well aware of its power, and did not hesitate to exploit it. She made full use of the glamour of her youngest daughter, Marguerite, as a means of impressing ambassadors to court, and she also employed what was called her 'flying squadron', a group of beautiful young girls of good birth who had two principal functions at court: the first, to attend on Catherine, but the second, and more important, to attend on any young men whom Catherine might happen to want either kept out of mischief or spied upon. In the most notorious instance of this, during the period when Catherine's son-in-law Henry of Navarre and her own youngest son Francis of Alençon were being kept virtual prisoners at the French court, both fell in love with the same girl—who, on Catherine's orders, acted as mistress to both, and dutifully reported back to the Queen Mother whatever she was able to learn from her two lovers. This was a technique which Catherine was to employ for the rest of her life, and one which she usually found highly successful.

She was also, however, prepared to encourage more ortho-dox alliances as a means of promoting her ends. Despite the small happiness that she herself had gained from being a bride in a diplomatic alliance, she enthusiastically pursued suitably splendid brides and bridegrooms for all her children. Occasion-ally she was forced to settle for less: her eldest daughter Claude found no grander husband than the Duke of Lorraine, and the wife who was eventually chosen by Catherine's favourite son Henry, Louise of Lorraine-Vaudémont, was also an unimpressive catch in diplomatic terms. She had more success, in dynastic if not in personal terms, with her son Francis and her daughter Elisabeth: each of them gained a crown—Francis that of the King Consort of Scotland, Elisabeth that of the Queen Consort of Spain. Ultimately, though, the marriages failed to achieve what had been hoped of them, for very few of Catherine's children equalled her own impressive fecundity. Elisabeth produced only daughters, who could not inherit the Spanish crown and so produce the permanent Franco-Spanish link which Catherine had hoped for; and Francis died childless, which meant that the crown of Scotland passed out of the hands of France.

Not deterred by these two failures, however, Catherine moved on to her two grandest marriage-schemes of all—for her youngest son, Francis of Alençon, and for her youngest daughter Marguerite. At first the Queen Mother had tried to retain the link with Spain that had been lost by Elisabeth's death by trying to persuade her widowed son-in-law Philip II to take Marguerite as his next wife; but the plan fell through when Philip refused to go along with it. So Catherine decided on the daring idea of using Marguerite in an attempt to patch up the religious differences between the Valois and their Bourbon cousins through a marriage between Marguerite and the Bourbon heir to the kingdom of Navarre. Once again, however, the Queen Mother's grand plans for a child of hers were frustrated by the child herself: the marriage proved not only childless but unhappy and ended in divorce.

Francis of Alençon, too, failed to fulfil his mother's schemes. For him, Catherine had plotted the greatest match of all: despite an eighteen-year age gap and different religious persuasions, she hoped to marry Francis to the most eligible matrimonial catch of the day, Elizabeth of England herself. Elizabeth does indeed seem to have conceived a certain fondness for the ugly, pockmarked little prince, whom she affectionately christened her 'frog', and seems at one time to have been within a hair's-breadth of contemplating marriage to him; but in the end she could not bring herself to go through with it, and the unfortunate Alençon died before any further plans could be hatched for him by his ambitious mother.

The problems met with by Catherine in her marriage plans for her children were paralleled by those she encountered in the political arena. Like Mary of Guise, Catherine de' Medici found herself in the invidious position of being a foreign, Catholic Queen in a country where there was a large and vociferous Protestant party. The marriage between her daughter Marguerite and the Protestant Henry of Navarre had been an attempt to deal with the growing split between the two parties; but it was to take more than a marriage to bridge such a huge divide, and history has never forgiven Catherine for her part in the St. Bartholomew's Massacre.

The coming of age of her son Charles IX officially meant that Catherine no longer exercised power, but Charles's poor health brought him to an early grave, and he was succeeded by Catherine's favourite son, Henry III. The strong affection between them meant that Catherine was able to retain considerable influence in the new reign; but there was little she or anyone could do to heal the wounds of religious difference which were rending France asunder. She continued planning and travelling well into old age, until news was brought to her that Henry III had imitated her own action of years before by ordering the murder of the Catholic leader, the Duke of Guise, and his brother. The Queen Mother was old and frail by now, and the news killed her—fortunately for her, as it turned out, for her own death only barely preceded that of her favourite son King Henry, stabbed to death in a revenge attack for Guise's murder. Catherine, who had devoted herself for so long to the advancement of her children, and had already seen so many of them predecease her, was at least spared that final sorrow.

If the destiny of her children was the major preoccupation of Catherine de' Medici, it was not a problem for Margaret of Austria, the first of the Habsburg Regents of the Netherlands. Margaret was the daughter of Mary of Burgundy, the fabulously wealthy heiress of the Low Countries, and of Maximilian, Archduke of Austria, who was later to become the Holy Roman Emperor Maximilian I. Their marriage was rare in that, although based initially on reasons of state, it appears to have developed into a genuine love-match; but the young couple's happiness was cut short when Mary, indulging in her favourite passion of hunting, was thrown from her horse and, having refused a medical examination to preserve her modesty, died of internal injuries some days later, at the age of only 24. She left her husband with two small children: Philip, who now became the Duke of Burgundy, and Margaret, who had been called after Mary's beloved stepmother Margaret of York. Mary's dying wish had been that her husband Maximilian should be allowed to govern as Regent for the young Philip, and pursue the series of successful campaigns that he had been waging against France for the return of the Burgundian inheritance in France, which had been confiscated by the French on the grounds that Mary, as a woman, could not succeed to it. The citizens of the Low Countries, however, did not wish to have any more war, with its deleterious effects on trade. Instead, their representatives removed the two ducal children from their father's care and, without Maximilian's consent, betrothed the little Margaret to the Dauphin of France as a pledge of alliance.

The young Archduchess Margaret was only 3, but it was nevertheless agreed that she was to travel at once to her new home in France, under heavy guard in case her father Maximilian should attempt to regain custody of her by force. She was received in France by the King's daughter, Anne de Beaujeu, who at once demanded to see the little girl undressed so that she could be sure that she was not in any way deformed. Once this test had been safely passed, Margaret was first of all betrothed to the Dauphin Charles, and then, the next day, married to him, though in view of the extreme youth of the new bride she was allowed, for the moment, to live alone in a separate household.

Many details survive of Margaret's life as Dauphine of France. She had a large staff, including, charmingly, a lavender-lady, and accounts still exist detailing the money that was spent on dresses for her dolls, food for her to give to the castle doves and to her pet parrot, and on the little lambskin coat that was supplied for her to wear in winter. She was a pretty child with red-gold hair, often set off by clothes of her favourite colour, the black that had been the traditional attire of her forefathers the Dukes of Burgundy. In other ways, however, her Burgundian and Austrian ancestry was ignored: instead of the German of her father's domains or the Flemish of her mother's, she was taught only French, the language of the country of which she was one day expected to be Queen.

Margaret's peaceful world was, however, shattered when she was 11 years old, by the death of Duke Francis II of Brittany. The heir to the duchy was the Duke's daughter, Anne, who immediately became the most eligible prize on the international marriage market. Margaret's father Maximilian hastened to propose to Anne; he was duly accepted and they were married by proxy. But Anne de Beaujeu, now Regent of France for her young brother Charles VIII, Margaret's husband, had no intention of seeing the important duchy of Brittany fall into the hands of France's enemy Maximilian. Instead, she invaded, forced Anne to rescind her promise of marriage to Maximilian, and decided that, in order to secure possession of Brittany for the crown of France, Margaret of Austria must be divorced and the young King Charles married to Anne of Brittany instead.

Utterly humiliated, Margaret, now an 11-year-old divorcee, declared herself too ashamed ever to return to her native Flanders; and indeed she did stay in France for two years, while her former husband haggled with her father over whether or not he would have to return her dowry. In the end he agreed to do so, because his plans for a campaign in Italy meant that he could not afford to alienate Maximilian any further, and Margaret, now 13, duly returned to the homeland she had not seen since the age of 3.

Not for long, however. Charles of France's Italian plans were merely a prelude to his grand design for launching a campaign to recapture the lost city of Byzantium from the Turks and have himself crowned its Emperor; and to frustrate these grandiose ambitions, Margaret's father Maximilian allied with Ferdinand of Aragon, who also, like Maximilian himself, had hopes of securing territory in Italy. The alliance was to be sealed by a double marriage between the two rulers' children: Maximilian's only son, Philip, Duke of Burgundy in the right of his mother, was to marry Ferdinand's eldest daughter Juana, and Margaret herself was to marry Juan, only son of Ferdinand and his wife Isabella of Castile and heir to both their kingdoms. Margaret, now aged 17, set off once again on her travels; no longer Queen of France, her destiny now seemed about to make her Queen of Spain instead.

Once again, however, her future proved unpredictable. After a crossing buffeted by storms, Margaret arrived in Spain to discover that her new bridegroom was a sickly boy of 19, who found himself so exhausted by the round of festivities which accompanied their marriage that his doctors begged his mother Queen Isabella to prevent him from sleeping with his new wife in case the strain should kill him. Isabella refused to interfere in the matter; but soon she was to regret her decision, for the doctors were proved right. Only five months after the marriage, Juan died.

Margaret was pregnant at the time, but her child, a daughter, was born prematurely, and did not live. After a two year sojourn with her bereaved parents-in-law in Spain, she returned once again to her native Low Countries, arriving just in time to be godmother to Charles of Ghent, the first son of her brother Philip and his wife Juana. Her father was anxious to use her for a third time in a diplomatic marriage, and suggestions for a husband for her included most of the potentates of the day: Louis XII of France, Duke Ludovico Sforza of Milan, James IV of Scotland, Prince Arthur of Wales, and Ladislav Jagellon of Hungary. In the end, however, the choice fell on Philibert, Duke of Savoy, nicknamed 'The Handsome'. His lands were not so extensive as those of many of the other princes who had been proposed for her; but in other ways he proved a very satisfactory choice. He was young, and had not for nothing been christened 'The Handsome'. Margaret fell in love with him, and was also delighted to discover that since Philibert himself took little interest in the business of government, he was very happy to let her take care of such matters for him. Showing an early aptitude for the business that would one day become her life's work, Margaret ousted from power her husband's illegitimate brother René, who rejoiced in the soubriquet of 'The Great Bastard', and took over the reins of government herself.

But her happiness was to be short-lived. One hot day three years after their marriage, Philibert grew restless for exercise, and despite the prevalent belief that exercise in hot weather was dangerous to the health, Margaret eventually gave in to his pleas and agreed that he could go hunting. He rode like one possessed and then, in spite of warnings from his nobles, assuaged the tremendous thirst he had built up with gallons of icy spring water. Almost immediately he was seized by acute pains in his side and had to be carried home in agony. Margaret was devastated; as once her father had done, when her mother Mary of Burgundy was dying, she made vows of prayers and pilgrimage, and in accordance with the medical wisdom of the time, gave her fabulous pearl necklaces to be dissolved into medicines for Philibert. But it was all to no avail. After a brief illness, Philibert died; his young widow had to be forcibly restrained from throwing herself out of her window, and sheared off all her hair in mourning. She kept his embalmed heart with her for the rest of her life.

The new duke, Margaret's brother-in-law, had no desire for her to remain in Savoy, and her own brother, Philip of Burgundy, rapidly began to make plans for her remarriage. This, however, Margaret would not consider. She refused to comply with the arrangements made by her father and brother that she should marry the recently-widowed Henry VII of England and, for the third time, went back to the Netherlands.

There seemed to be little future for her there, or for that matter anywhere. If she would not listen to offers of remarriage, she would be condemned to remain a widow, with no place or power, and with no rôle in life. Perhaps, however, Margaret took courage from the example of her godmother, Margaret of York, who, after the death of her husband Duke Charles the Rash of Burgundy, had refused all suggestions of marriage to stay in her adopted duchy and render political assistance to her stepdaughter Mary. For Margaret of York, however, there had at least been that task to fulfil; for Margaret of Austria, there seemed to be nothing that she could do—until, once again, death took a hand in her story.

Two years after the death of Philibert, Margaret's brother, Philip of Burgundy, insisted, despite all advice, on playing a vigorous ball-game after a heavy dinner, and then, like his brother-in-law before him, quenching his thirst with draughts of spring water. Again, the combination of the vigorous exercise and the icy water proved fatal.

Philip's wife, Juana, had always been mentally unstable, and now the death of her husband unhinged her totally. She was therefore unable to do anything to protect the position of her son Charles, who now, at 6 years old, became Duke of Burgundy. His grandfather Maximilian was declared Regent for him, but he was busy enough governing his own ancestral territories of Austria and the Holy Roman Empire, and could hardly rule Burgundy as well. What was needed was someone on the spot, someone who knew the Low Countries well enough to be able to govern them with tact and sensitivity and who could also command authority amongst the people. Margaret, daughter of the Netherlands' Duchess Mary and sister of their last Duke, was the ideal choice.

The news of her appointment was greeted with great enthusiasm by the inhabitants of the Low Countries, and Margaret rewarded their confidence in her by rapidly demonstrating that she intended to take her task seriously, governing not just in the interests of her father but also in those of her subjects as well. She also devoted herself to the bringing-up of her little nephews and nieces, virtually orphaned now that their father was dead and their mother an imprisoned lunatic. Until her death in 1503, the Dowager Duchess Margaret of York had cared for the children; now four of them, Eleanor, Charles, Isabeau and Mary, aged from 8 to 1, came to Margaret, while Ferdinand, the second boy, was brought up by his maternal grandfather Ferdinand of Aragon, and Catalina, born after the death of her father, shared her mother's melancholy captivity in the gloomy tower of Tordesillas. As well as busying herself with the children, Margaret, like her mother before her, indulged her lifelong passion for pets: she kept dogs, guinea pigs and a parrot. She took care, too, to surround herself with the splendour which was so old and famous a tradition of the Burgundian court; she entertained poets and musicians, kept a famous choir, and had her apartments decorated with paintings by the Low Countries artists Memling, Van Eyck, Van Der Weyden and Bosch. And, as an investment for the future when her nephew Charles would grow up and be able

149

to rule his domains for himself, she persuaded her father to give her lands in the Empire and to create her Countess of Burgundy.

Margaret proved a careful and able Regent. She secured a favourable trade agreement with England, and she was also able to persuade her father Maximilian to discontinue the long war he had been fighting against Guelderland, which had been having a bad effect on Low Countries trade. The citizens were so grateful to her for this that they voted her a special gift of £60,000, a very considerable sum in sixteenth-century terms.

Since trade formed so vital a part of the Netherlands' economy, Margaret, like her father Maximilian, adopted a pro-English policy. Her dealings with the touchy Henry VIII of England had won her quite a reputation as a diplomat; but they did not please her young nephew Charles, in whose name she was governing, since his pro-French tutor had taught him to dislike and distrust the English. Charles was, too, offended when his aunt showed disrespect for that most revered of all Burgundian institutions, the Order of the Golden Fleece. Despite her own Burgundian ancestry, Margaret failed to understand the power and prestige of the Knights of the Fleece: she regarded orders of chivalry as a costly waste of time, and on one occasion declared to the assembled knights, 'Ah, sirs! If I were such a man as I am a woman, I would make you bring your statutes to me and sing out bits of them!' Such an attitude did nothing for her popularity in the protocol-conscious Burgundian lands, and Margaret's position was also undermined when her father Maximilian struck a secret deal with France without informing his supposed ally Henry VIII. Henry was naturally furious; Maximilian, safe in Austria, was too far away to feel the effects of his wrath, but Maximilian's daughter Margaret could be made aware of it via the wool-trade with England which was such a vital part of the Netherlands' prosperity.

At this most delicate of junctures Margaret's father struck her another unexpected blow when he suddenly declared Charles, now 15, old enough to govern for himself. Charles had been less than enamoured of his aunt's behaviour of late, and he soon gave her to understand so. Her influence dwindled rapidly and rumours began to fly that during her Regency she had governed unwisely and with an eye mainly to her own profit. Her period of disgrace did not last long, however. The next year her former father-in-law, Charles's maternal grandfather, Ferdinand of Aragon, died. His heir, in theory at least, was Charles; but since Charles was then in the Low Countries, there was a move in Spain to place his younger brother, another Ferdinand, on the throne instead of him, so that Spain would not have to suffer the indignity of being ruled from a distance. Charles would have to go to Spain in person to be sure of his inheritance, and had no one other than Margaret whom he could reasonably appoint Governor of the Netherlands in his absence. Moreover, the Emperor Maximilian had discovered that his grandson was less willing to take his advice than his daughter had been, and so he, too, backed the move for Margaret's return to power.

At first Margaret was given only a co-governorship with a Council of the Knights of the Golden Fleece. Within a year, however, she had been placed at the head of the Council and awarded the power to sign all state papers, as well as being given a pension of the then large sum of £20,000. She also busied herself with the attempt that was currently being jointly mounted by Charles and Maximilian to ensure that after the latter's death Charles would be able to succeed him as Holy Roman Emperor. The main means of conducting this campaign was by heavy bribery of the seven German potentates who had the power of electing the Emperor; and since Charles soon discovered that his grandfather had an unpleasant habit of embezzling the money sent to him for this purpose, he began increasingly to trust Margaret with the distribution of the bribe-money. In 1519 the sudden death of Maximilian made the matter more urgent, and also more complicated when two rival candidates, Francis I of France and Henry VIII of England, entered the lists. Knowing that they too would be dependent on bribes to conduct their campaigns, Margaret forbade the town of Antwerp to lend any money to foreigners, thus effectively depriving them of a major potential source of loans. Charles won the campaign, and, partly as a reward for her loyalty and assistance, he restored to Margaret her title of Regent of the Netherlands.

Nor was this the end of her services to him: it was Margaret who finally resolved the long drawn-out war between Charles and the French King Francis I by arranging to meet Francis's mother Louise of Savoy, sister of her own beloved husband Philibert, at Cambrai, where between them they negotiated the end to hostilities which became known as the Ladies' Peace. It was, however, the last of her achievements. She was already 49 years old, no longer young in sixteenth-century terms, and in great pain from a suppurating leg. The next year, she died.

She was succeeded, after a gap of a year, by her niece, Mary of Hungary, younger sister of the Emperor Charles. Like most of the children of Philip and Juana, Mary had been brought up first of all by the Dowager Duchess Margaret of York, and then by Margaret of Austria herself, so she was familiar with the Netherlands and well suited to govern them. At the age of 7, Mary had been betrothed to Louis Jagellon, heir to the Hungarian throne, and in due course had married him, while her brother Ferdinand had married Louis' sister Anne. Mary's marriage had been a brief one, however; in 1526 the Turks invaded Hungary and her young husband was killed fighting them at the Battle of Mohacs. Since he and Mary had no children, the claim to the throne passed to Mary's sister-in-law, Anne, and her husband, Mary's brother Ferdinand. Mary left it to them to attempt to fight off the Turks who were now the *de facto* rulers of the kingdom; she herself returned to her native Netherlands, and was thus on hand to take up the government on the death of her aunt.

Mary of Hungary was an astute and able woman and also had the added advantage, which her aunt had not, that her brother, the Emperor Charles, was very fond of her and did not feel for her the shadows of distrust that had dogged his relationship with Margaret. Mary governed the Netherlands steadily and well, and also kept up the Burgundian custom of governing with magnificence; in 1549, when she had been Regent for eighteen years, she played hostess to her nephew Philip, only son and heir of the Emperor Charles, and staged for him some festivities at her castle of Binche which were talked of for years afterwards as the bench mark for all other entertainments of their kind. Nor was serious business neglected during Philip's visit; staying in the Netherlands for two years, he had ample opportunity to learn about the people of these lands which would one day be his, and to learn about the political institutions there. He must have been satisfied with what he saw, for when the Emperor Charles abdicated in 1555, leaving Philip in power, Mary was still retained as Governor. Three years later, however, she died—in the same year as Charles himself, and also in the same year as their elder sister Eleanor, the widowed Queen of France.

Mary of Hungary was lucky in that her period of governorship in the Netherlands fell before the worst of the religious troubles which were eventually to split the provinces. The same could not be said of the next female Governor, Margaret of Parma. Margaret was the illegitimate daughter of the Emperor Charles by a Low Countries woman, and was therefore, like Margaret of Austria and Mary of Hungary before her, a member of the royal family and a native of the Netherlands. Although illegitimate, she was nevertheless openly acknowledged as Charles's daughter and Philip's half-sister; she was married to the Duke of Parma, to whom she bore a son, Alexander Farnese, who was later to succeed her as Regent of the Netherlands, and she was always called by the title Madama (of Parma). After the death of her husband, she returned from Italy and was installed by her half-brother Philip, now King Philip II of Spain, as Regent of the Netherlands.

Margaret of Parma, however, was not to have so easy a time of it as her aunt and great-aunt had done. As in many places elsewhere in Europe, there was growing agitation in the Netherlands for Protestant Reform, something which Philip II, the Most Catholic King, would never countenance. There was also pressure for political independence; for over half a century now the Netherlands had been used as pawns to further their rulers' interests elsewhere, and the effects on trade had not been good. Moreover, although the Emperor Charles had at least been born in Ghent and had spent much of his youth in the Low Countries, Philip II was more Spanish than Flemish, and was seen in the Netherlands as, to all intents and purposes, a foreigner. Margaret of Parma did her best, but it was hardly surprising that, in the situation, she failed to make much headway.

The crisis of her administration came when, in 1565, the Count of Egmont, a prominent Low Countries politician, travelled to Spain to put his and his colleagues' grievances in person to Philip II. Philip was deeply worried by problems elsewhere in his vast territories and had no wish to spend time talking to Egmont, and he therefore took a very unwise decision: he made up his mind to appear sympathetic to Egmont, so that the Count would go away happy, but not in fact to commit himself to any kind of reform or change. The Count was convinced by Philip's soothing words and returned to the Low Countries, where he promptly spread word that concessions were about to be granted. No sooner had the rejoicing begun at the good news when a packet of letters arrived from the King in Spain completely contradicting the news that Egmont had just brought and indicating that Philip's attitude remained as uncompromising as ever.

Margaret of Parma wrote to her brother for guidance but none came; Philip was still occupied by other problems and seems to have preferred not to think about the hornets' nest that he had inadvertently stirred up in the Netherlands. By the time he turned his attention to the problem, Margaret of Parma was no longer in any doubt about how to act; faced with a deputation of armed men who had marched into her palace and confronted her with their demands, she had had no choice but to accede to them, and to order the suspension of the laws used to prosecute Protestants as heretics. Soon afterwards a further and more important concession, full toleration for Protestants, was wrung from her.

In response to her increasingly desperate appeals for assistance, Philip now decided to act. He publicly endorsed what his sister had done, but he also sent her authorization and money for the raising of mercenary soldiers. He sent, too, an army of his own, headed by the disciplinarian Duke of Alva, perhaps in the belief that since Margaret of Parma, a mere woman, had failed to assert her authority, Alva, a man and a soldier, would be able to do so instead. At all events, this military intervention meant that Margaret's career as Governor of the Netherlands was, effectively, over.

Alva, however, failed, to make a better job of it than she had done. Indeed, his brutality only fanned the flames of the Low Countries' resistance. After Alva, a succession of Spanish governors was tried in turn: Don Luis de Requesens, Philip II's illegitimate half-brother Don John of Austria, and finally Margaret of Parma's son Alexander Farnese, Duke of Parma. None was able to restore peace and tranquillity to the troubled provinces; the halcyon days of the Low Countries, under the rule of Margaret of Austria and Mary of Hungary, had gone for ever.

Another woman who, during the course of the sixteenth century, succeeded in exercising power as a Regent was Louise of Savoy, sister-in-law of Margaret of Austria and mother of the French King Francis I. Louise had never been a Queen; her husband had been Charles of Angoulême, and she had been given to him as a punishment for what his sovereign, Louis XI of France, saw as his inordinate ambition in having aspired to the hand of Mary of Burgundy, richest heiress of her day. At the time of the betrothal, Charles was 18, but Louise was only 1, so that not only was he to be disappointed of his hopes of the Duchess Mary, but would be forced to wait a very long time before he could acquire a wife and the hopes of a family. He had some hopes of being allowed to break his engagement with Louise and find himself another wife; but when it was discovered that he was involved in a plan to marry his cousin the Duke of Orléans to another wealthy heiress, the Duchess Anne of Brittany, he was once again punished, this time by the ratification of his marriage to Louise.

Despite this less than promising start, the marriage was a perfectly successful one, largely because Louise immediately became great friends with her husband's mistress. It produced two children before her husband's early death— Francis and a daughter, Marguerite, so christened because her mother had swallowed a pearl (in Latin, *margarita*), during her pregnancy. Louise was devoted to both her children, but especially to her son: she referred to him as 'my Caesar', and to the family together as 'the Trinity'. Marguerite, too, a clever girl later to become famous as the authoress of the *Heptameron*, adored her brother, and it was later said that Francis was 'born between two women on their knees'. Louise watched devotedly over the education of her family; she even arranged good marriages for all her late husband's bastards, and where her own two children were concerned her care knew no bounds. Her tireless efforts were finally rewarded when, on the death of his cousin Louis XII, her son became King Francis I of France.

Louise still did not relax her vigilance. It was she who is said to have warned Francis that if he continued his attentions to the widowed Queen, Mary of England, he might just succeed in fathering a child which would actually take precedence in the succession before him; and it is also said to have been she who warned Francis that he could not afford to divorce his wife Claude and risk the concomitant loss of her Duchy of Brittany. Louise really came into her own, however, after what might well have been the greatest disaster of her life: the capture of her beloved son Francis by the Spanish, after the Battle of Pavia in 1524. Louise at once stepped into the breach and with admirable rapidity and efficiency organized fund-raising for the ransom, while herself functioning as Regent until the money had been gathered. She also set to work on her former sister-in-law, Margaret of Austria, the aunt of Francis's captor the Emperor Charles. One of the main demands which Charles was making was the return to him of the Duchy of Burgundy, confiscated by the French in the previous century on the grounds that Mary of Burgundy, as a woman, could not succeed to it. One way in which Charles had hoped to exert pressure for the return of the Duchy was by military action from the adjacent County of Burgundy, which, since it was in territory governed by the Empire rather than by the French crown, had been split off from the Duchy and was now being governed by Philiberte of Luxemburg, Princess of Orange, in the name of Margaret of Austria, who had been made Countess of Burgundy by her father the Emperor Maximilian. Margaret of Austria duly signed a treaty with Louise promising that the County would never wage war on the Duchy, thus depriving the Emperor Charles of a valuable potential weapon.

Louise also worked to forward the marriage between Francis and the Emperor's sister, Eleanor of Austria, which she saw as a potential way to end the hostilities between the two. To this end she arranged a further collaboration with Margaret of Austria, when the two met at Cambrai, with Louise's daughter Marguerite also in attendance, to seal the 'Ladies' Peace', which guaranteed the safe return of the French princes, held hostage for their father in Spain, and the marriage of Francis with Eleanor of Austria. This was, however, to be Louise's last service to her son, for like Margaret of Austria, she died the next year.

The French historian Michelet once referred to Anne of Brittany, Margaret of Austria and Louise of Savoy as 'the three Fates working together for the ruin of Europe'; but it can equally well be asserted that by their resolute deployment of power and by their reliance on marriage and diplomacy rather than on war, Louise and Margaret, at least, had done much to save Europe.

VI

Queens Who Might Have Been

IF there were many women who succeeded in achieving the rank of Queen in the sixteenth century, there were also several who might have done so but failed. Prominent amongst these were two heiresses of the House of York, Elizabeth, daughter of Edward IV, and Margaret, daughter of the Duke of Clarence. There two women were cousins, since George of Clarence, father of Margaret, was the younger brother of Edward IV, father of Elizabeth.

Edward IV had come to the throne in 1461, after a prolonged struggle between his father, Richard, Duke of York, and the reigning Lancastrian King, Henry VI. The roots of the conflict between the two men went back to the deposition of Richard II in 1399. Richard had been the only son of Edward the Black Prince, the eldest son of Edward III, and as such he had succeeded to the throne on his grandfather's death in 1377 as undisputed heir. He had, however, failed to produce a son, and he had, in addition, lost the support of many prominent noblemen, so in 1399 he was deposed by his cousin, Henry Bolingbroke, who thus became King Henry IV. Bolingbroke's right to the throne was not undisputed, however. He claimed it through his father, John of Gaunt, third son of Edward III; but the second of Edward III's sons, Lionel of Antwerp, had also produced a child. The problem was that Lionel's child had been a daughter, Philippa.

Richard II himself, before his deposition and eventual murder, had declared that he wished the succession to pass to the descendants of Philippa. That, however, was now overruled; Philippa, as a woman, was deemed ineligible to transmit the succession (despite the fact that Edward III himself had earlier claimed the crown of France through his mother and that his descendants continued to assert this claim through the female line). Lionel of Antwerp's line was thus passed over and the crown vested in Henry IV.

As far as Philippa's descendants were concerned, however, that was not the end of the matter, and their claim to the throne was, in their own eyes, made even stronger by the fact that Philippa's daughter, Anne Mortimer, had married her cousin, Richard, Earl of Cambridge, who was himself descended from Edmund Langley, Duke of York, fourth son of Edward III. At the death of Anne Mortimer's only brother, her son, Richard, Duke of York, inherited the combined claims of both his parents. Because of his title his was known as the Yorkist claim, while Henry IV and his descendants, because of their claim from the Duke of Lancaster, were known as Lancastrians.

During the lifetime of the strong Lancastrian Kings Henry IV and his son Henry V there was little scope for designs on the crown. But when Henry V died in 1422 he left as his heir a baby, and there followed an inevitable troubled period during the minority of the young Henry VI. Even when the King grew to manhood he did not exercise strong government, because he was by temperament a pious man little interested in temporal affairs, which he was prepared to leave largely to his wife, Margaret of Anjou, and her associates. This dominance by the Queen effectively excluded Richard of York from power. At first he was prepared to tolerate this, since the royal marriage was childless and he himself was therefore the heir to the throne; but when the Queen produced a son, Edward, who ousted him from this position, York moved to claim the power he felt he had been unjustly denied.

A prolonged period of hostilities resulted, during which neither side was able decisively to establish superiority. York's claim was by now no longer for just a share in the government; he was openly demanding the disinheritance of Edward, Prince of Wales, and his own recognition as heir to the throne. Margaret of Anjou would never countenance such a disregard for the rights of her son and when, after some years of intermittent conflict, she captured York and his young son the Earl of Rutland, she showed no mercy. Both were killed on the battlefield, and York's head, with a paper crown around its temples, was publicly displayed on the battlements of his own city of York.

His claim to the throne passed immediately to his eldest son, Edward, the Earl of March, who, at only 18, was already a seasoned and successful general. The young Earl of March had better luck than his father, and shortly after the death of York, Edward of March obtained his revenge for the executions of his father and his brother when he and his two remaining brothers, George and Richard, defeated the royal army at Tewkesbury. Edward, Prince of Wales, was killed in the battle and this, together with the defeat itself, sounded the death-knell for the Lancastrian hopes. The young Earl of March was crowned Edward IV, and his two brothers George and Richard became Dukes of Clarence and of Gloucester respectively. Although there was a brief resurgence of the Lancastrian cause in 1470, when the Lancastrian King Henry VI was temporarily restored to the throne and Edward IV was forced to flee to his sister in Burgundy, he soon regained his throne, and kept it until in 1483, although still a relatively young man, he died.

The death of Edward IV opened the way for a power struggle. Edward had made a controversial marriage: instead of following the precedent of his ancestors by taking a foreign princess as his Queen, he had married, for love, Elizabeth Woodville, the widow of an English knight who already had children from her first marriage. Although Elizabeth was connected through her mother with the Burgundian ducal family, she was widely regarded as an upstart, and so at the death of Edward she found herself largely friendless. She and Edward had produced two sons, Edward and Richard, but they were both still children. A regency would therefore have to be established, and the late King's youngest brother, Richard of Gloucester, capitalized on the Queen's unpopularity to have himself declared Lord Protector. Once he had established himself in power, he went further. Declaring that his two young nephews were illegitimate because Edward IV had previously been contracted to another woman before he married Elizabeth Woodville, he imprisoned them in the Tower of London and had himself proclaimed King Richard III. The two boys were never seen again, though whether they died of natural causes, by the order of Richard himself, or by the order of his successor King Henry VII, has never been established.

The two princes had not, however, been the only children of Edward IV and Elizabeth Woodville. There were also numerous daughters; and the removal from the public stage of her brothers now lent the eldest of these, called Elizabeth after her mother, a particular importance, since she could perhaps be considered the legitimate heiress to the throne. Although she herself, as a woman, was not considered as a potential ruler in her own right, it was nevertheless possible that whichever man she married would be able to claim the throne through her; and rumours began to spread that King Richard, recently widowed, was anxious to subvert any such attempt by marrying Elizabeth himself, although she was his niece. Another candidate, however, was also interested in her hand: Henry Tudor, Earl of Richmond.

Henry Tudor's mother, Margaret Beaufort, was a descendant of John of Gaunt, third son of Edward III, through whom the Lancastrian Kings had claimed the throne. The Beaufort family were in fact the product of John of Gaunt's relationship with his mistress, Katherine Swynford (sister-in-law of the poet Chaucer), and since Katherine Swynford had not become Gaunt's third wife until after the birth of their children, the Beaufort claim, being based on illegitimate descent, was not a strong one. During the lengthy conflict between the Houses of Lancaster and York, however, all those members of the Lancastrian family with a claim superior to the Beauforts' had been killed, so that now Margaret Beaufort was the only remaining representative of the Lancastrian claim; and she, as a woman, had stepped aside for her only son, Henry. At the defeat of the Lancastrian cause he had been taken by his uncle, Jasper Tudor, to safety across the channel in Brittany; now, however, the insecurity of Richard III's reign, coupled with the fact that the King had no son to succeed him, seemed to augur well for any attempt to revive the fortunes of the Lancastrians. Henry in Brittany began to lay his plans, while his mother in England seems to have negotiated with the widowed Elizabeth Woodville for the hand of her daughter, the Yorkist heiress Elizabeth.

In 1485 Henry Tudor landed at Milford Haven, in his native Wales, and marched to meet Richard's army. The two clashed at Bosworth, in Leicestershire. Richard's forces were defeated; he himself was killed during the course of the battle. The last Yorkist King was dead and Henry Tudor duly succeeded as Henry VII.

To bolster his new position Henry was determined to do two things: he wanted to marry Elizabeth of York, both to boost his own claim to the throne by the addition of hers and also to prevent her from marrying any other possible husband who would be a potential threat to him; but at the same time he was anxious to make it plain that he was claiming the throne because of his own descent from Edward III rather than in the right of his wife. He therefore had himself independently declared King before announcing his marriage, so that Elizabeth became merely his Queen Consort rather than in any sense Queen in her own right.

Elizabeth of York herself seems to have acquiesced happily enough in all these arrangements, and made no attempt to play any part in the government of the kingdom or in political affairs. When her eldest son was born, he was, significantly, not given the Yorkist name of Edward, which would have stressed his ancestry on the mother's side, but the Welsh one of Arthur, which was intended to capitalize on the Welsh descent of his father and on the splendour of the Arthurian legends; a second son was named Henry after his father, and the third, Edmund, after his Tudor grandfather, while the eldest daughter was named Margaret after Henry's mother Margaret Beaufort. Elizabeth of York's own ancestry was celebrated only in the myth which began to grow up around the Lancastrian-Yorkist conflict as a War of the Roses—a title which seems not to have been used before the Tudor period but which then rapidly became widespread. According to this, the followers of the Lancastrian claimants had adopted as their badge a red rose, and the Yorkist supporters a white one; and the marriage of Henry and Elizabeth was therefore presented as the union of these two roses into a single one, the Tudor rose, with mingled petals of both white and red.

This attempt to present Elizabeth of York as the embodiment of the White Rose may have been, at least in part, an attempt to obscure the inconvenient fact that there were actually other representatives of the House of York still alive. Elizabeth's aunt, another Elizabeth of York who was a sister of the Yorkist Kings Edward IV and Richard III, had married John de la Pole, Duke of Suffolk, and had borne him a son, also called John, who had been declared by Richard III to be the heir to the crown and who became popularly known by the title of 'The White Rose'. His claim, however, was only through the female line; even stronger was that of the Earl of Warwick, who had been the only son of George, Duke of Clarence, the younger brother of King Edward IV. Clarence had been committed to the Tower for treason by King Edward, and had died there—according to some, drowned in a butt of malmsey on the orders of his younger brother Richard of Gloucester, afterwards Richard III—and his son too had been a prisoner in the Tower from an early age. Possibly as a result of his long incarceration, he appears to have lost his wits; but this did not deter some from regarding him as the rightful King of England. Early in the reign of Henry VII one Lambert Simnel impersonated him and led a rebellion, and even after this had been suppressed the name of Warwick continued to be a focus for discontent, until Ferdinand of Aragon, alarmed at the disturbances generated in favour of the unfortunate young man, made his execution a condition of the marriage of his daughter, Katherine of Aragon, with Henry VII's son Arthur, Prince of Wales.

The death of Warwick did not, however, exhaust the list of possible Yorkist claimants, for he had a sister, Margaret, who had been created Countess of Salisbury in her own right and given in marriage to Sir Richard Pole. Margaret became a great friend of Katherine of Aragon, partly because of the guilt the latter felt at learning that she herself had unwittingly been the cause of the execution of Margaret's brother. The two shared a staunch Catholicism, and their children—Katherine's daughter the Princess Mary Tudor and Margaret's son Reginald Pole—were childhood playmates who, their mothers seem to have hoped, might one day marry. Like many royal women who stood in the line of succession, the Countess of Salisbury seems to have seen herself rather as a transmitter than an inheritor of royalty, focussing her ambitions on her children rather than on herself; but that was not to save her when, in the later years of his reign, Henry VIII's darkening temperament drove him to attempt to purge all those whom he saw as possible threats to the secure continuation of his dynasty. Although she was by now 80 years old, the Countess of Salisbury was condemned to death by beheading. As Queen Anne Boleyn had indicated in her urgent desire for a skilled swordsman to behead her, Tudor executions could be messy businesses: it took the inept executioner several blows to head, neck and body before the last Yorkist princess gave up the ghost.

The careers of other royal women also demonstrate how perilous it could be to be a potential transmitter of the royal blood. King Henry VIII had always preferred his younger sister, Mary, to his elder one, Margaret, and he had therefore declared in his will that the children of Mary were to be given preference in the succession over those of Margaret, coming directly after his own son and daughters. This was a provision which was eventually to be disregarded when, in 1603, the crown passed to Margaret's great-grandson James VI of Scotland; but until then it hung dramatically over the lives of Mary's two daughters, Frances and Eleanor, and their children. The elder daughter, Frances, had been married to Henry Grey, Marquis of Dorset, and bore him three daughters, Jane, Catherine, and Mary; and when in 1553 it became apparent that the young King Edward VI was seriously ill and could not live long, the thoughts of the ambitious noblemen who surrounded him began to turn to the succession. The legal heir, according to the will of King Henry VIII, was Edward's elder half-sister, Katherine of Aragon's daughter Mary; but Mary was a Catholic, and the Protestant lords who had prospered under Edward VI feared that if she came to the throne they would suffer loss of favour and would possibly even have to return the monastic lands that they had acquired in the reign of Henry VIII.

If Mary was passed over, however, then the succession would pass next to the eldest daughter of Henry VIII's younger sister, Lady Frances Brandon, now Duchess of Suffolk; and the Duchess and her husband were well known to be sympathetic to Protestantism and to have brought their three daughters up in that religion. The Duchess herself seems to have been an arrogant and unpleasant woman, who dominated her rather weak-willed husband; and their eldest daughter, Lady Jane Grey, said that both her parents were cruel and unsympathetic to her, interested only in how she could help them fulfil their ambitions. Certainly they were quick to respond when the suggestion was made to them by John Dudley, Duke of Northumberland, that if they would allow their daughter Jane to marry Northumberland's son Guildford Dudley, and if the Duchess would further renounce her rights to the succession in favour of her daughter, then it might be possible to stage a *coup* which, after the death of King Edward VI, would put Guildford and Jane on the throne as King and Queen of England. Despite Jane's own protests, the marriage was performed, and the young King Edward was persuaded, in the interests of Protestantism, to declare his cousin Jane his heir.

Lady Jane herself seems to have had no ambitions to become a Queen. When the crown was offered to her, she declined, saying that it was rightfully the property of her cousin Mary; but what Jane thought was, of course, of no account. Although it was she who had been declared the heir by King Edward, and she who was of the royal blood, Northumberland's plan was in fact that Jane should declare her husband Guildford King Consort, and that he himself would then exercise effective power through Guildford. Once again, the woman was thought of as merely a transmitter of power, rather than a repository of it; and the fact that if Mary was to be set aside at all, then the rightful heir should really have been Frances Brandon herself rather than her daughter was conveniently overlooked in the plans laid by Northumberland and by Jane's parents.

The fact that Jane was intended as a mere figurehead did not, however, save her when growing support for Mary and defections among Northumberland's party brought the end of her nine-day reign. Jane, Guildford, Northumberland and Northumberland's four other sons were imprisoned in the Tower to await the pleasure of the new Queen Mary. In the case of Northumberland there could be no doubt; as the main instigator of the plot, he was beheaded. Queen Mary was inclined to show mercy to Jane and to Guildford on the grounds that Jane was her cousin, that they were both very young (only 16) and that they had been puppets in the plot rather than prime movers of it; but constant pressure to the contrary was placed on her by the Spanish ambassador, who had been sent to her by her prospective husband, her cousin Philip of Spain. The ambassador argued that as long as Jane was alive she would provide a focus for possible unrest, and his words appeared to be proved true when Jane's father, the Duke of Suffolk, made an unsuccessful attempt to lead a rising in her favour. Suffolk was executed, and so was Jane's husband Guildford. Jane herself lived long enough to see her husband's headless corpse being carried underneath her window before she too was beheaded.

The penalty paid by Lady Jane Grey was, however, avoided by her mother. Perhaps as a reward for having refrained from asserting her own rights to the succession and declaring herself Queen, or perhaps because the executions of her husband and her daughter were considered punishment enough for her, Frances Brandon escaped the general downfall of her family, and lived to defy convention by marrying, only three weeks after her first husband's death, her much younger steward. Nine months after the wedding she gave birth to another daughter, but the child died in infancy, before the Tudor blood she had inherited from her mother could be to her the problem it had been to her older sister Jane—and would be, too, to Frances Brandon's two surviving daughters from her first marriage, Lady Catherine and Lady Mary Grey.

Like her sister Lady Jane, Lady Catherine Grey was to suffer for her place in the succession. After the death of Queen Mary Tudor in 1558, the late Queen's half-sister Elizabeth came to the throne. Elizabeth was the last of the children of Henry VIII; and she was still unmarried and, therefore, childless. Lady Catherine was thus one of her very few close relatives, and, according to the will of Henry VIII, her heir. But Elizabeth had no desire for people to be focussing on the successor to the throne rather than on its current occupant, and was therefore not inclined to look with favour on Lady Catherine, who was after all the sister of a former usurper.

Elizabeth's fondness for Lady Catherine was by no means increased by the discovery that Philip of Spain, despairing of persuading Elizabeth to convert to Catholicism, had hatched a plot to kidnap Lady Catherine and marry her to his heir, Don Carlos, with a view to installing the young couple as joint sovereigns on the English throne. This prospect of a virtual replay of what had happened with Lady Jane Grey and Guildford Dudley by no means appealed to Elizabeth.

Lady Catherine seems to have been well aware of the delicacy of her own position and of the possibility that, since any husband of hers could be potentially so dangerous to Elizabeth, she might well never be permitted to marry at all, or at least not until the Queen had settled down with a husband and children of her own, something of which there seemed no immediate likelihood. Unfortunately, Lady Catherine was not prepared to endure the probability of a long wait until she could obtain permission to marry, for she had fallen in love.

The young man of her choice was Edward Seymour, Earl of Hertford, whose father, the Duke of Somerset, had been uncle and Lord Protector to King Edward VI until he had been executed as a traitor as a result of the machinations of his enemy the Duke of Northumberland. The disposal of Somerset had been the first stage in Northumberland's campaign, which had eventually culminated in the marriage between his son Guildford and Catherine's sister Lady Jane. Since the execution of Somerset, the Seymour family had been in eclipse; young Edward Seymour had not been allowed to inherit his father's title of Duke of Somerset, being merely Earl of Hertford instead, and it was not likely that Elizabeth would look favourably on a proposed marriage between the son of one executed traitor and the daughter and sister of two others. But Hertford and Catherine were in love, and took the rash step of deciding to marry secretly and trust to Elizabeth to come round to the idea in due course.

Time, however, was not on their side. They had not been long married when Hertford was ordered abroad, and Lady Catherine discovered to her horror that she was pregnant. Since her condition would soon be impossible to conceal, the Queen would have to be told at once.

Elizabeth's reaction to the disclosure that the heir to the throne had contracted a secret marriage and was about to bear a child was fury and outrage. Hertford was recalled from France and sent straight to the Tower; Lady Catherine was confined there too, and in due course gave birth to a son. Since being the mother of a male heir would serve to strengthen Lady Catherine's position as heir, Elizabeth was further angered by this development; and her fury increased still further when, as a result of conjugal visits illicitly allowed by the Lord Lieutenant of the Tower, a second son was born to the offending couple. Since the marriage had been performed in secret, however, neither the Earl nor Lady Catherine was able to prove that it had actually taken place: the only witness, the Earl's sister Lady Jane Seymour, had since died, and the priest who had performed the ceremony could not be traced. Elizabeth therefore seized on the one opportunity still available to her and declared that since there was no proof of the marriage the two children were illegitimate. Although Lady Catherine was eventually released from the Tower into the custody of her uncle, she died soon after of consumption.

The third Grey sister, Lady Mary, had a career less tragic than that of either of her sisters, but infinitely more pathetic. She seems to have suffered from some form of restricted growth syndrome, and was also hunchbacked. She appears to have had a kindly nature, however, and in spite of her unfortunate physical appearance she attracted the admiration of one Thomas Keyes, who was a sergeant-porter at one of the Queen's palaces. He proposed to Mary and she accepted. As in the case of her sister Lady Catherine, they were secretly married; but once again, the secret came out—much to the amusement of all the court, for Thomas Keyes' immense height made a bizarre contrast to the tiny Lady Mary. There was also a dark side to the laughter, though. Since the death of her sister Lady Catherine and the bastardizing of the latter's children, Lady Mary was now, under the terms of Henry VIII's will, next in line to the throne; and as such she could hardly be allowed to throw herself away unpunished on a mere sergeant-porter. Perhaps because she had not committed the additional crime of further complicating the succession by producing children, she was spared the Tower, but was put in the custody of relations. Her husband was imprisoned, and died soon after; Lady Mary's pathetic request to be allowed the care of his children by his first marriage was not granted, and she herself died a few years later, without having married again.

The descendants of Lady Frances Brandon's younger sister, Eleanor, were further from the forefront of politics by virtue of the fact that they came lower in the succession than Lady Frances and her daughters. Lady Eleanor had married Henry Clifford, Earl of Cumberland, and had borne him one daughter, Lady Margaret Clifford, who married the Earl of Derby; and although the presence of Tudor blood in his family tree was rumoured to have caused the death of Ferdinando Stanley, Margaret Clifford's eldest son, she herself and her mother Lady Eleanor had lived out their lives in relative peace. This was not the case, however, for another woman with the blood of the Tudors, Lady Arabella Stuart.

Lady Arabella was descended from Lady Margaret Douglas, the daughter of Henry VIII's elder sister Margaret, Queen of Scotland, by her second marriage to the Earl of Angus. Lady Margaret's parents divorced when she was young and she herself was brought up at the English court, under the eye of her uncle King Henry VIII, where she was popularly though erroneously known as the Princess of Scotland. After various intrigues surrounding the question of possible husbands for her, she was eventually married to Matthew Stuart, Earl of Lennox, and became the mother of two sons, Henry and Charles. The elder of these two boys, Henry, Lord Darnley, became the ill-fated second husband of Mary, Queen of Scots, and father of her only son James, eventually meeting a mysterious death in which Mary herself may or may not have been implicated; and there was also a connection between Mary, Queen of Scots, and the marriage of the younger son, Charles.

At the time of Charles's marriage Mary was in England, a prisoner of her powerful cousin Queen Elizabeth. She had been put in the charge of George Talbot, Earl of Shrewsbury, who had married as his second wife the formidable Elizabeth

Hardwick, who was later to become known to history as 'Bess of Hardwick'. Bess had worked her way up through the social scale through a series of four marriages, each grander than the last, culminating in that to Talbot which had made her Countess of Shrewsbury. Bess's twin ambitions centred on the numerous building projects which she pursued and on the advancement of the children of her second marriage, to Sir William Cavendish. At the time of her fourth marriage to the Earl of Shrewsbury she had also arranged that her own second son, Henry Cavendish, should marry the Earl's daughter, Lady Grace Talbot, while Bess's daughter, Mary Cavendish, married Gilbert Talbot, Shrewsbury's son. But when Bess encountered Lady Margaret Douglas, the possibility of a still greater match presented itself to her. Together, the two women agreed that Lady Margaret's surviving son Charles Stuart should marry Bess's daughter, Elizabeth Cavendish.

Bess of Hardwick had been the daughter of a badly-off gentry family, and such a marriage represented a tremendous advancement for her family. It made her daughter Elizabeth the sister-in-law of Mary, Queen of Scots, great-niece by marriage of Henry VIII and aunt by marriage of the ruling King of Scotland, James VI; and even more importantly, it could also give any children who might result from this marriage a place in the succession to both the English and the Scottish thrones. This was in fact a fairly remote possibility; but Bess's immense ambition may well have made it seem to her more likely than it actually was that a grandchild of hers might one day wear a crown. Queen Elizabeth's angry reaction to the news of the marriage, which led to the imprisonment of both Bess herself and also of Lady Margaret Douglas, served to confirm the political importance of the marriage. But however significant an alliance it might have been in dynastic terms, it was a short-lived one, for soon after the birth of the couple's only child Lady Arabella, Charles Stuart died. His young widow followed him to the grave soon after and the orphaned little girl was brought up by her formidable grandmother Bess.

Bess's ambitions for the little Arabella, whom she termed 'my jewel', seem to have known no bounds. As soon as the death of her fourth husband, with whom she had quarrelled,

freed her to use her funds as she liked, she began the building of the splendid Hardwick Hall, a new house adjacent to
the older one in which she had been born. The entire upper
floor was given over to rooms suitable for being used on a
grand state occasion—particularly, a visit by a Queen. Bess
is unlikely to have thought that the ageing Queen Elizabeth
would travel so far north to favour her with a visit; it seems
more probable that the rooms were designed for occupation
by a putative Queen Arabella, although the decoration of
them was based round a theme which would be suitably
pleasing to Elizabeth if she should ever get to hear of them
or see them.

But while it was easy enough to build state rooms in happy
anticipation of the event of Arabella's hoped-for succession,
it was much less easy to engineer the succession itself.
Elizabeth was notoriously averse to naming her heir, and in
any case informed observers thought it much more probable
that she would disregard the terms of her father's will and
would confirm the succession on her cousin, James VI of
Scotland. What made matters worse was that if Arabella
was not sufficiently well placed in the succession to be the
obvious candidate for Elizabeth's heir, she was nevertheless
too highly placed in it to be allowed to marry at will. Arabella
herself seems to have found this restraint irksome and even
to have gone so far as to scheme behind her grandmother's
back to procure herself a husband. It is unclear whom she
had in mind; some rumours said that it was Robert, Earl
of Essex, the favourite of the Queen, but it may also have
been Edward Seymour, Lord Beauchamp, the son of the
ill-omened marriage between the Earl of Hertford and Lady
Catherine Grey. At all events, the Queen discovered the
plans and acted swiftly to frustrate them, confining Arabella
to the restrictive care of her irate grandmother.

When Elizabeth I did eventually die in March 1603, the
succession passed, as had been widely expected, to James VI
of Scotland, whose father Henry, Lord Darnley had been the
elder brother of Arabella's father Charles Stuart. King James
took something of a fancy to his cousin, and although he
refused to grant her grandmother's long-standing request
that Arabella should be allowed to inherit her father's title as

Countess of Lennox, he did allow her considerable freedom and privileges, which were not rescinded even when, in 1605, a plot was mounted by Roman Catholics, aided by some of Arabella's male relatives, to put her on the throne. The death of her grandmother, in 1608, freed Arabella still further from restraint; unfortunately, however, she did not make wise use of her freedom. Whether or not he had indeed been the subject of her earlier marriage intrigues, she now came to an understanding with Lord Beauchamp that they should marry in secret and flee to France to be out of the way of the King's wrath. Such a marriage was doubly dangerous. Although King James had children of his own, and Arabella was thus no longer immediately in line for succession to the throne, she was nevertheless the King's cousin, and as such needed his permission to marry; and matters were further complicated by the fact that Arabella's prospective husband, Lord Beauchamp, was himself the bastardized son of the earlier secret marriage between Lady Catherine Grey and the Earl of Hertford. As Lady Catherine's son, he too, under the terms of Henry VIII's will, had a claim to the throne; his mother had been the legal heiress, and if his father had succeeded in his lifelong campaign to have the legitimacy of his marriage recognized then Lord Beauchamp might well have been able to put up a strong case for his own succession. The union of these two possible Pretenders was something that King James was likely to take very seriously indeed.

Undaunted, the young couple set off for France; but although Beauchamp arrived in safety, Arabella was captured on the voyage. She was brought back to England and imprisoned in the Tower of London. Her descent from Lady Margaret Douglas had already blighted her life; now it was to do so still further, since Lady Margaret had inherited from her mother, Queen Margaret Tudor, the royal disease of porphyria. This had already manifested itself in Queen Margaret Tudor's son, James V of Scotland, and his daughter, Mary, Queen of Scots; one of its principal symptoms, an agonizing pain in the side, had been troubling Arabella for a long time, and now her condition began to deteriorate. Like another Tudor descendant, King George III, two centuries later, she lost her reason, and died.

Lady Arabella Stuart was not the only royal woman who succumbed to madness: as we have seen, the same fate afflicted Juana of Castile. Juana, eldest daughter of Ferdinand of Aragon and Isabella of Castile, had an unfortunate family history. Her maternal grandmother, Isabella of Portugal, had run mad and had been incarcerated in a castle under strict supervision, and both Juana's great-grandson, Don Carlos, and her great-great-grandson, Dom Sebastian of Portugal, were to display clear signs of mental instability. Juana herself began to show symptoms of mental trouble during her marriage to Duke Philip of Burgundy. But after his sudden death she lost control completely, and was incarcerated in the tower of Tordesillas.

However personally unfortunate, Juana's madness was in many ways politically convenient. The death of her only brother Juan shortly after her marriage had left her the heiress to her parents' kingdoms of Aragon and Castile; and this was a situation with serious problems attendant upon it. In the first place, it was by no means clear that a female would be allowed to succeed in Aragon, which eventually led King Ferdinand, after the death of his first wife Isabella, to marry again in the hope of producing a son who could secure the succession. In Castile, the fact that Queen Isabella was herself a woman meant that there could, of course, be no problem with a female succession; but since it was universally accepted that it would not be a Queen but her husband who wielded effective power, even there the succession of Juana was viewed with some concern, because the Burgundian and Austrian ancestry of her husband Philip meant that he was viewed as unlikely to be sympathetic to the interests of Castile. Ferdinand and Isabella in particular did not like or trust their daughter's husband; at the time when they had married her to him, Juana had not been the heiress of Spain because her brother was still alive, so they had had no idea that they were picking their own eventual successor, and perhaps would have chosen a very different son-in-law if they had.

In 1504 Isabella the Catholic fell mortally ill. She tried to make provisions for the succession which would somehow exclude her unsatisfactory son-in-law from power, and in her will she begged that Ferdinand might be allowed to continue governing Castile as Regent for Juana. But the Castilians had never been particularly fond of Aragonese Ferdinand, whom they regarded as a foreigner from a lesser state, so Isabella's will was ignored and Ferdinand himself was forced to return to his own kingdom of Aragon. Power was transferred to his daughter and his son-in-law: she now became Queen Juana of Castile, with King Philip I as her consort.

For two years Philip ruled Castile in the name of Juana, and, in the view of Ferdinand and indeed of the Castilians themselves, did not make a particularly good job of it. If Juana herself was devastated by the sudden death of her husband two years after her accession, her father was delighted; he immediately returned to Castile, on the pretext of taking care of his daughter, and when he discovered her condition he acted at once. He persuaded the Castilians to allow Juana to be locked up and Ferdinand himself to function as Regent in the name of Charles of Ghent, eldest son of Philip and Juana, still only a child of 8.

Indeed, Juana's madness was so convenient for her father's political ambitions that there were some who refused to believe in its existence, or at least its extent. King Henry VII of England had met Juana when she and Philip had been driven ashore on the English coast and had therefore been forced to spend some time with him at Windsor; he had been much taken by her beauty then, and now that he and she were both widowed he put in a request for her hand in marriage. When it was objected that she was mad, he airily replied that that was of no importance as long as she was still capable of bearing children. Henry's remark has often been interpreted as a piece of crass insensitivity; but it may perhaps also have been intended to express a doubt as to whether Juana was really mad at all, or locked up merely in order that her father could rule. It would certainly have been a spectacular political coup for Henry if he could have got Juana into his hands, as his wife, and had then been able to declare that she was restored to sanity, and would have been a tremendous embarrassment to his long-time opponent Ferdinand.

It was not only Ferdinand, however, who had an interest in seeing Juana stay in Tordesillas. The madness of Juana meant that the vexed question of female succession in Aragon need never, in practice, arise, since the next ruler of Aragon after Ferdinand would now be his grandson, Juana's son, Charles. When Ferdinand did indeed die in 1516 Charles, now 16 and able to rule in his own right, at once came south from the Netherlands to take possession of his new Spanish territories. Nominally, he was co-ruler with his mother; but in practice, of course, he exercised sole power, and had no desire to relinquish any of it. Like another son of an imprisoned mother later in the century, James VI of Scotland, Charles had no reason to wish to see his mother emerge from her prison to deprive him of any of his authority. Indeed, there were even rumours that whenever Juana showed any signs of an incipient return to sanity she was beaten until she lapsed into acquiescence; and it was certainly true that frequent beatings formed a part of her régime, and were personally approved by Charles. She was allowed the companionship of her youngest child Catalina, who had been born after the death of Philip, but otherwise the lunatic Queen dragged out an isolated, comfortless and loveless existence in her prison for many years, not dying until 1555, the year of her son's abdication.

Given the heavy price that could be attendant on Queenship, it was hardly surprising that some women, such as Margaret of Austria and Christina of Denmark, Duchess of Milan, actually turned down the opportunity to become Queens, refusing offers of marriage from the English Kings Henry VII and Henry VIII respectively, while both Lady Frances Brandon and her sister and niece showed no interest in asserting any rights they might possibly have had to the throne. Although a woman might find opportunities to exercise power as the wife of a King or, still more easily, as the mother of one, to attempt to rule as Queen in her own right was a dangerous business with few chances of success and considerable possibility of disaster. And if disaster did indeed occur, there was the added disadvantage that femininity, though it could be such a major obstacle in the pursuit of power, provided no protection if power was not achieved. For a woman who tried and failed, despair and death waited.

VII

Queens Regnant

DESPITE the failure rate amongst would-be queens, however, a small number of remarkable women did succeed in exercising power in their own right. Isabella of Castile in Spain, Jeanne d'Albret in Navarre, Mary and Elizabeth Tudor in England and Mary, Queen of Scots, in Scotland all with varying success and for varying lengths of time won acknowledgement as women rulers.

Within this small group can be detected different attitudes towards the idea of independent female power. For some of these women, the idea of ruling in their own right, without help from a man, was virtually unthinkable. Isabella of Castile was anxious to associate her husband Ferdinand with all her actions, and greatly disliked taking or even appearing to take decisions independently of him. Although she participated to the full in his attempt to reconquer the Moorish-held territories of southern Spain, and even went so far as to appear in front of the troops in armour, she saw her own rôle very much as that of interceding with God through her prayers rather than actively directing combat, although she does in fact seem to have been a perfectly competent general. She also insisted on the most rigorous standards of sexual conduct amongst her own ladies, and was herself a model of chastity (indeed, the purity of her personal life coupled with her persistent attempts to initiate programmes of evangelization among the American Indians have led to repeated and recently revived calls for her canonization); at the same time, however, she appears to have been prepared to tolerate her husband's philandering (in a way that her daughter Juana most definitely was not when it came to Philip). Isabella was a Queen Regnant who was very much prepared to take second place to her husband.

To some extent the same was true of Mary Tudor, who succeeded her half-brother Edward VI on the throne of England in 1553. Despite a protected and cosseted child-hood, surrounded by skilled tutors, a loving mother and a proud father, Mary had gone on to experience a bitterly unhappy girlhood: her mother Katherine of Aragon had been slandered and divorced by her father Henry VIII, who had further threatened both Katherine and also Mary herself with death, and she had, too, been forced to witness the wrenching away of England from what she regarded the true faith of Catholicism to the false one of Protestantism. Even when the death of her brother left her the legal heir to the crown, she still had to face out the rebellion of the Duke of Northumberland before finally, at the age of 37, she became Queen Mary I.

Until the time of her accession she had never been able to marry. As a girl she had been betrothed to the Dauphin of France, but that had come to nothing when, as a result of her parents' divorce, her father had declared her illegitimate; and for the rest of his reign, and also for that of her Protestant half-brother Edward, she had been largely in disfavour. Now, however, it was assumed by the Queen and her people alike that she would marry. Power might have devolved on her, but naturally she would transfer it to a responsible male. As an angry crowd had cried in the time of Henry VIII at the news of Katherine of Aragon's imminent divorce, 'They would have no King but the Lady Mary's husband.'

The difficulty was the choice of husband. Her earlier, childhood betrothal to the Dauphin had generated consider-able unease, for if the marriage had taken place it would have meant that England would have been effectively absorbed by France—exactly the situation which threatened when Mary, Queen of Scots, was simultaneously Dauphine of France and Queen Regnant of Scotland. Marriage to a native English-man could prove equally problematic if the Queen's choice of one noble over the others were to excite jealousy and create factions; and to make matters worse, there was by no means an abundance of suitable foreign princes from whom she could choose. Mary, however, had no need to hesitate, for she had already decided on her husband. Once, as a girl, she had been betrothed to the Emperor Charles V, the nephew of her beloved mother; he was a widower now, and nearing the end of his life, but he did have a son, Philip, who was of marriageable age. Although the Spanish prince was some years younger than Mary, it was nevertheless agreed that he should marry her.

The match was deeply unpopular in England. The unrest that had only recently died down, with the quelling of the rebellion in favour of Lady Jane Grey, now flared up again; in the years since the Reformation England had learned to mistrust and fear Spain, and few people now wanted to see a Spanish King Consort on the English throne. But Mary put down the rebellion and pressed on with her plans. After so many years of bitterness and neglect, she intended to let nothing spoil her chances of happiness.

Unfortunately, however, Philip did not bring her happiness. He found it difficult to deal with her fondness for him, and their childlessness strained the marriage. In English eyes, Philip was also implicated in Mary's decision to engage in hostilities with France, with which Philip's native Spain was at war, and this led to the disastrous loss of Calais, the last of the English possessions in France and therefore of immense symbolic importance. Mary, frustrated as a wife, unable to become a mother, died after only five years on the throne declaring that she had 'Calais' engraved on her heart. Nor was this the only blot on her public image: she left behind her black memories of the persecution of Protestants which she had undertaken in order to bring England back to what she saw as the true path of Catholicism, but which were to earn her the name of 'Bloody Mary'.

The difficulties of choosing a suitable husband were also vividly illustrated by the troubled marital career of Mary Tudor's cousin, Mary Queen of Scots. The political difficulties attendant on her marriage to the Dauphin might well have proved immense; to have been Queen Consort of one country and Queen Regnant of another, separated from the first by a sea, would have been difficult rôles for the young Mary to combine for a long period. On the other hand, Mary's career after her return to her native Scotland demonstrated that in the question of a husband for a Queen Regnant, there was no easy answer. As in the case of Mary Tudor, she risked exciting jealousy if she showed such a signal favour to a member of her native nobility; yet a foreign husband would be regarded with distrust. Many suggestions were made, including one from Elizabeth I who made the bizarre offer that Mary could have as her husband Elizabeth's own favourite the Earl of Leicester. In the end, however, Mary chose for herself, and for love. She married her cousin Henry, Lord Darnley, and declared him King Consort of Scotland.

Mary had fallen for Darnley while she was nursing him during what was probably an attack of the measles. She may well have been influenced by his handsome looks (she was also said to have been anxious to find a man who could match her own height of six feet, and Darnley was tall); but he also had suitable ancestry, since his mother had been Lady Margaret Douglas, daughter of Margaret Tudor, Queen of Scotland, and half-sister of Mary's own father King James V. Unfortunately, Darnley's personality soon proved a singularly unsuitable one for the demanding and delicate rôle of King Consort. He was grasping, easily led, temperamental and subject to fits of jealousy, pique and sulks. Mary, who may perhaps have pandered to him at first, soon seems to have lost patience with him; she was attempting, with some tolerance, to grapple with the highly sensitive religious situation in Scotland (she, like her cousin Queen Mary Tudor, had the disadvantage of being a Catholic Queen in a predominantly Protestant country) and she needed men made of sterner stuff than Darnley to help her. The climax in their relationship came when Darnley, at the head of a band of armed men, burst into a room in the pregnant Queen's private apartments and stabbed to death her favourite Italian musician, David Rizzio, in front of her, on the almost certainly false grounds that he was her lover. It says much for Mary's strength of mind that she rose to this ghastly situation and was able to wheedle Darnley away from the side of his co-conspirators to escape with her. But once she was safely away from danger Mary's attitude appears to have hardened. She may have been prepared to humour Darnley when she needed his help, but she could no longer like or trust this vain and vicious young man. Few of those who continued to support her could have been in any doubt about her feelings for her husband, and not long after the death of Rizzio, Darnley too was found murdered.

Whether Mary herself had any part in his death has been much debated and can probably never be established with certainty. Whether she was innocent or not, however, there were plenty of people opposed to her religion and her policies who were very ready to believe in and to proclaim her guilt; and certainly appearances were against her when, soon after the murder, Mary announced that she had married for a third time, and that her new husband was James Hepburn, Earl of Bothwell, who was widely considered to be the chief suspect for Darnley's murder.

Bothwell was a nobleman of an ancient and prominent family who had been a supporter of the policies of Mary of Guise, Mary's mother and Regent, and of Mary herself. If, as seems highly probable, he was indeed involved in the murder of Darnley, his motives are debatable; and the reasons for his next move are equally unclear. Perhaps his actions were motivated by personal ambition; perhaps he was acting out of some bizarre form of loyalty or even love; perhaps he was genuinely convinced that he was the best man to help Mary and that she must be made to see so. At all events, it now seems fairly clear that Bothwell, probably without Mary's connivance or foreknowledge but just possibly with it, abducted the Queen. He then, almost certainly, raped her.

Mary, who appears to have feared that she had become pregnant as a result of the rape, had little choice but to marry him. Bothwell seems to have thought that he would be able to protect her from the ensuing political storm; but in this he was to prove mistaken. Popular Protestant preachers whipped up hatred of the Queen as an adulteress, a whore and a murderess, and there were mounting cries for her abdication in favour of her infant son James. Several of her leading nobles took arms against her, assisted by Mary's able half-brother Lord James Stewart, an illegitimate son of King James V; Mary and Bothwell were unable to muster sufficient troops to fight them, and at Carberry Hill the unhappy couple were forced to surrender. Bothwell was exiled abroad, where he died insane in a Danish prison, and Mary herself was first made to abdicate and then confined on an island in Loch Leven, where she may perhaps have suffered a miscarriage of twins, presumably as a result of the rape.

After her recovery from her various ordeals, she began to gather her spirits again, and was eventually able to contrive her escape from Loch Leven. Her freedom was short-lived, however. Unable to rally support in Scotland, she made the rash decision to flee to England, in search of assistance from her cousin and fellow-Queen, Elizabeth Tudor. Elizabeth, however, was perfectly happy with the Protestant government that had been set up in Scotland following Mary's abdication, which was headed by Mary's illegitimate half-brother the Lord James, and had no desire to see it replaced by a Catholic régime under Mary. Nor did she want Mary at liberty in England, where she would provide a natural focus for the discontent of English Catholics unhappy with the Protestant government of Elizabeth herself, and would also be a centre for the intrigues which normally clustered around the heir to the throne, as they had around Elizabeth herself in the days of her sister Queen Mary Tudor. Mary was therefore declared Elizabeth's prisoner and detained first in Carlisle Castle, and afterwards in various other residences in the north of England.

If this was an unpleasant situation for Mary, it was also by no means a comfortable one for Elizabeth. The mere fact of Mary's imprisonment did not deter plots from forming around her, which provided considerable headaches for the Elizabethan government; and Elizabeth came under some pressure to put her cousin to death. This, however, she was reluctant to do. To behead a Queen Regnant, even one who had been deposed, was a dangerous precedent, which she had no desire to institute in case it might be one day applied to herself; so Mary was allowed to live on in captivity, where she involved herself in various schemes to secure her release and, if possible, place her on the English throne. One of her principal bargaining-cards in these was her own person: once her third husband Bothwell had met his miserable end in the Danish dungeon of Elsinore, she was free to marry again, and was not short of prospective candidates for the position of her fourth husband, including Don John of Austria and also, much to Elizabeth's chagrin, the English Queen's premier courtier and cousin, the Duke of Norfolk. Mary's attraction as a possible bride was of course due partly to the fact that she could lay claim not only to the throne of Scotland but also, if Elizabeth was deposed, to that of England; but in one respect, too, her captivity worked to her advantage, for it meant that tales could still circulate of her enchanting grace and beauty, unhampered by the reality of increasing plumpness and loss of hair that enforced lack of exercise and prolonged ill-health had brought upon her.

Eventually, the persistence of conspiracies around the imprisoned Queen of Scots and the worsening political and religious situation in England persuaded Elizabeth reluctantly to agree to Mary's execution on the grounds of the plots she had helped hatch against Elizabeth's life and throne. She was beheaded at Fotheringhay Castle in 1587, and passed immediately into legend as a figure of a romance and glamour which survive to this day, though few in her own country appear to have regretted at the time the death of a woman who had been popularly branded as both murderess and whore.

Another Queen who suffered from an unfortunate choice of husband was Jeanne d'Albret, heiress of the tiny Pyreneean kingdom of Navarre. Jeanne was the daughter of Henry d'Albret, King of Navarre, and his talented wife Marguerite, sister of King Francis I of France, widow of the Duke of Alençon and authoress of *The Heptameron*. D'Albret had married Marguerite largely in the hope that her brother King Francis would help him recover the Navarrese territories which had been invaded by Ferdinand of Aragon, and when he was disappointed in this relations between the royal couple deteriorated rapidly. Marguerite was deeply interested in the new religion of Protestantism, and her husband disapproved; on one occasion when he found her praying with ministers of the Reformed faith he slapped her in front of them. Henry and Marguerite also fell out about the marriage of their only child, Jeanne. Henry, in his ceaseless quest to regain the lost lands of Navarre, hoped to marry Jeanne to Philip of Spain on condition that he and she should rule jointly over a restored Navarre; but Marguerite's brother Francis I was anxious to avoid anything which might increase the powers of the Spaniards, and so proposed an alternative alliance for the young heiress with the Duke of Cleves. Henry d'Albret actually begged the Spanish to kidnap his daughter so that she could be married to Philip, and Queen Marguerite was placed under considerable pressure by both her husband and her brother to advance their respective plans.

Eventually, Francis I moved to enforce his will and marry Jeanne to the Duke of Cleves, and Henry and Marguerite were forced to acquiesce. Francis came up against an unexpected obstacle, however, in the shape of Jeanne herself. Although only 12, she made her displeasure clearly known, and even when she was eventually forced to go ahead with the betrothal, she signed a statement saying that it was against her wishes. As a result of these protests, and of the changing political situation, the Pope was persuaded, two years later, to annul the marriage on the ground of non-consummation, and to the displeasure of her parents but to her own great delight, Francis married her to Anthony of Bourbon, a prince of the blood royal. The marriage seemed to start well—Bourbon announced to a friend that he was 'doing his marital duties day and night'—and in due course produced two children, a son, Henry, and a daughter, Catherine (it was rumoured that, as a demonstration of her stoicism, Jeanne's father insisted on her singing a madrigal while in labour). In due course Henry d'Albret died, and Jeanne and Anthony succeeded him as King and Queen of Navarre.

The new Queen faced a delicate political situation. As well as the question of the lost territories which had so troubled her father, she also had to deal with an attempt by her cousin, Henry II, now King of France, firstly to pressure Jeanne and Anthony into trading some of their most valuable lands for others that he tried to offer them, and then, when that failed, to take their principal citadel of Navarrenx by treachery. Such actions did not bode well for the political future of Jeanne and Anthony; and Anthony, at least, as a prince of the blood, had ambitions for political success. Since it seemed unlikely that he would be allowed much participation in the government of France, his attentions turned in another direction: towards the Reforming preacher and politician John Calvin, leader of the Protestant city of Geneva. If he could not shine in government, he could at least achieve primacy amongst the growing band of French Protestants.

Anthony of Bourbon's own adherence to Protestantism was a tenuous one, fluctuating with the various changes of the political wind. His wife, however, was much more whole-hearted in her conversion to the new faith. In 1560, after the first signs of trouble had broken out between French Protestants and Catholics, she publicly announced her new religion and from then on she, together with Bourbon's brother the Prince de Condé, was the effective leader of the French Calvinist party. When she passed through Orléans on her way to Paris, twenty-five nuns escaped from their convent to hear her speak on the topic of Calvinism. Soon she had made herself so noted for her eloquence and her determination that when the Colloquy of Poissy was mounted to reach agreement between the two warring factions, the personable Cardinal of Ferrara was sent to attend it with the specific brief of distracting the female Calvinists, especially Jeanne, by his charm.

Jeanne herself was immune to such blandishments; her husband, however, was not. A timely offer from Philip II of the crown of either Tunis or Sardinia seduced Anthony from his allegiance to Calvinism and even made him contemplate divorce from his obdurate wife (he seems to have had designs on Mary, Queen of Scots). Jeanne was banished from her own court, and her son Henry was taken from her care; but almost immediately the first of the civil wars between Catholics and Protestants broke out, and Anthony was shot in the shoulder while publicly relieving himself outside the besieged town of Rouen as a gesture of his contempt for its defenders. He died a month later.

Jeanne was now free of her troublesome husband, and could proceed with her chosen tasks of fighting the cause of Calvinism and preparing her son Henry to succeed her. As a defender of Protestantism she proved so effective that Philip of Spain, having failed in an attempt to persuade her to marry a Spanish prince, actually planned to kidnap her and hand her over to the dreaded Inquisition for punishment. His plan failed, however, and Jeanne, remaining at liberty, began, despite considerable opposition, on a programme of forcible introduction of Calvinism into all her territories. She also helped her brother-in-law Condé with his military campaigns, both personally—when one of the most important of the Protestant mercenary captains had to have his arm amputated, Jeanne held his remaining hand throughout the operation—and financially, assisted by loans of money which Elizabeth I of England made her on the strength of her jewels. Despite Jeanne's importance to the rebel cause, the Queen Mother, Catherine de' Medici, was very reluctant to move publicly against her; she attempted unsuccessfully to dissuade the Pope from excommunicating her, and she also adopted the polite fiction of declaring that Jeanne was an unwilling prisoner in the Protestant camp rather than an active leader there. Ever reluctant to close doors, Catherine also mounted her campaign to persuade Jeanne to agree to a marriage between her son and heir, Henry, and Catherine's own daughter, Marguerite of France. Jeanne raised many objections to this—she insinuated her contempt for Catherine's banker ancestry, and also demanded, unsuccessfully, that Marguerite should be raised as a Protestant—but Catherine dealt patiently with all her protests, and also applied a bit of moral blackmail by hinting that if Jeanne would not comply, then the Pope would declare Henry illegitimate on the grounds that Jeanne had previously been married to the Duke of Cleves and that the marriage had never been properly annulled. Faced with such a barrage of persuasions, Jeanne eventually agreed to the marriage and went to court to discuss it.

There she was extremely unhappy. She considered the Valois court to be the most corrupt environment possible; she was not at all pleased about her future daughter-in-law's extensive use of make-up and elaborate styles of clothes and hair; and she was sure she was being spied on, even alleging that holes had been drilled in the wall of her room. She told her son Henry that the prolonged strain and difficulty of the marriage negotiations was taking a severe toll on her health—and she was right. She suddenly fell prey to a serious illness and died four days later, still aged only 44. Although poison was suspected at the time, her death is now usually attributed to a combination of the tuberculosis which afflicted so many members of the Valois family and an untreated abscess in the breast.

If Mary Tudor, Mary Queen of Scots, and Jeanne d'Albret all suffered for their choice of husbands, Elizabeth I's position was very different. When Elizabeth succeeded to the throne at the age of 25 she was, unlike her half-sister Mary before her, still attractive and still very much of marriageable and child-bearing age. She had also, however, been a witness of the disastrous marital career of her father (including the execution of her own mother) and had seen at first hand the political unpopularity and personal failure of her late sister's marriage. She was, therefore, very well aware of the risks incumbent on marriage; and she also knew that marriage and consequent pregnancy could bring, at worst, death in child-birth or, at best, a serious lessening of political importance. These reflections can only have been given added point by the ample opportunity afforded her, during the early years of her reign, to observe from a distance the matrimonial mistakes of her cousin and fellow-Queen, Mary, Queen of Scots.

There was certainly no shortage of candidates for the hand of Elizabeth. The King of Sweden was so smitten with her mere reputation that he bombarded her with gifts and threat-ened to come and woo her in person; her former brother-in-law, Philip of Spain, also proposed to her, and additionally offered that if she rejected him she might care to consider his cousin the Austrian Archduke Charles. In France, Catherine de' Medici, ever eager to pursue her policy of matrimonial diplomacy, eagerly pressed the successive candidatures of her two younger sons Anjou and Alençon, and the latter, despite being eighteen years younger than the Queen, con-tinued to pay earnest court to her until she was in her fif-ties. But both French princes, and the Spanish and Austrian candidates too, suffered from the grave disadvantage that they were Catholics and Elizabeth was Protestant, which was likely to lead both to political difficulties within the marriage and also to serious problems with the bringing up of any resultant children. This did not apply to the Lutheran King of Sweden, but on the other hand marriage to him would have put Elizabeth into the near-impossible position of attempting to function as Queen Consort of his country and Queen Regnant of her own, and was therefore out of the question. The problem was in any case solved for her when the King, tiring of his fruitless suit of her, first outraged his nobles by taking to wife the daughter of a common soldier, and then lost his senses and had to be imprisoned and deposed.

There were also some native English candidates for the position of King Consort. One who appears to have attracted some support was Elizabeth's cousin, the Earl of Huntingdon, a staunch Protestant and upright man of suitably royal descent; but she herself was far more attracted to Robert Dudley, Earl of Leicester, a younger son of the Duke of Northumberland who, in Edward VI's time, had schemed to put Lady Jane Grey on the throne, and brother of Guildford Dudley who had briefly become Lady Jane's husband. For a while Robert Dudley seemed set fair to match his brother's achievement by becoming the consort of a Queen Regnant, and one, at that, who had a much better chance of holding on to her kingdom than the unfortunate Lady Jane had had. But if Elizabeth herself had fallen victim to Dudley's charm, the greater part of her Council, including her most trusted adviser William Cecil, most definitely had not, and it even seemed probable that Cecil might resign if Dudley were to be elevated to the position of King Consort. Moreover, Dudley was already married; and when his wife, Amy Robsart, was found dead at the foot of a staircase, wild rumours flew that she had been pushed to her death to make way for a marriage between Dudley and the Queen. This was almost certainly not the case—Amy Robsart was probably suffering from breast cancer, and her death is now thought to have been due to a spontaneous fracture of the spine—but Elizabeth could not afford to be associated with such a scandal. If she was in any doubt as to what might happen if she married Dudley, she had only to look across the border to Scotland, where the conseqences of Queen Mary's marriage to Bothwell illustrated only too vividly the likely fate of a Queen who allowed herself to be tainted by a whiff of sexual scandal.

Gradually, therefore, as both foreign and domestic suitors failed to prove satisfactory, the possibility of Elizabeth's marriage faded from the horizon, and as time wore on and she came to the end of her childbearing years, her court and parliament even ceased to press her to consider the idea. Instead Elizabeth's own personal charisma and the elaborate court culture that she was at pains to foster began to produce a new and remarkable image for her: the Virgin Queen.

Virginity had long been considered to be possessed of holy, semi-magical powers. Mediaeval bestiaries told tales of the power of virgins to attract the legendary unicorn to lay its horn in their laps; this in turn was interpreted as being an allegory of Christ, unique like the unicorn, who had consented to place himself in the lap of the Virgin Mary and be born. The English Reformation had eventually led to a considerable downgrading in the status of the Virgin Mary and of other female saints, who also tended to be virgins; and this appears to have led to a considerable sense of loss and deprivation amongst Elizabethan women, robbed of possible rôle models and intercessors with heaven. This gap Elizabeth herself was ideally placed to fill. By emphasizing her virginity, she could associate herself indirectly with the Virgin Mary and also, directly and more decorously, with the virgin goddesses of classical mythology; and she could also distance herself completely from the suggestion of sexual incontinence which had dogged the careers of so many other female rulers, from Juana of Naples to Mary, Queen of Scots, and even the pious Mary of Guise herself. The weakness of woman was traditionally supposed to reside in her vulnerability to her own passions and her sensual nature; by becoming the Virgin Queen Elizabeth could transcend any suggestion of such weakness and even turn the problem of her gender into a positive advantage by drawing on the strands of mediaeval and chivalric thought which had elevated and deified women. She could capitalize, too, on the freak of Latin gender which had made so many abstract nouns feminine, and which had therefore led to the traditional personification of the virtues as female in mediaeval allegory.

So Elizabeth took the disabling and problematic fact of her own femaleness and transformed it into her greatest asset, becoming the ethereal, semi-divine Lady of chivalric tradition and courtly love presiding over her adoring knights. To what extent the process was a deliberately planned one, and to what extent it arose naturally, is difficult to say, but the model of Knight and Lady certainly provided a usable framework in which court culture and the business of government could both be conducted and the splendour of the Queen's image preserved, despite the distressing realities of her actual physical ageing. She became the Phoenix, unique because virgin; and during her forty-five year reign she completely transformed the image of the female ruler, changing the idea of a woman on the throne from a political and dynastic liability to a means whereby deep psychological needs could be satisfied and hidden sources of loyalty and devotion tapped. One of her most potent symbols was the pelican, which in mediaeval thought was regarded as a symbol of Christ because it was widely believed to tear its own flesh to feed its young on its flesh and blood, as Christ had done when he instituted the communion supper. Elizabeth was thus presented as simultaneously Christ-like and also as the mother of her people, sacrificing herself for their good. By refusing actual biological motherhood she had become in one sense the symbolic mother of England—the mother who was also a virgin, as the Virgin Mary had been.

Superlative as Elizabeth's mythological persona was, however, even it could not quite obscure the unpleasant actualities of the later part of her reign: the costly war with Spain, the bad harvests which led to widespread hunger and suffering, the Essex rebellion which aimed to put a young, active man on the throne instead of an elderly and often indecisive woman. When the old Queen finally died in 1603 and was succeeded by James of Scotland, son of Mary, Queen of Scots, there was widespread rejoicing at the accession of a King after fifty years of female rule, and foreign observers commented that they did not think the English would ever again allow themselves to be governed by a woman. Soon, however, the tide was turning the other way again. The court of James was corrupt and dissolute, and people soon began to wish for their Virgin Queen again; and within a very short period after her death her reign had become established in the popular imagination as a Golden Age, a character which it still preserves. Elizabeth, last and most successful of the women rulers of the sixteenth century, had served to establish on a secure foundation the possibility and legitimacy of female government, and also to illustrate that a Queen could reign on her own, without the help of a man, and might indeed be all the more successful for so doing.

Index of Principal Persons Mentioned